CW01654154

ANCHOR BOOKS

IN THE NAME OF LOVE

First published in Great Britain in 1993 by
ANCHOR BOOKS
1-2 Wainman Road, Woodston,
Peterborough, PE2 7BU

All Rights Reserved

Copyright Contributors 1993

Foreword

Anchor Books is a small press, established in 1992, with the aim of promoting readable Poetry to as wide an audience as possible.

We hope to establish an outlet for writers of Poetry who may have struggled to see their work in print.

Following our request in the National Press, we were overwhelmed by the response. The poems presented here have been selected from many entries. Editing proved to be a difficult and daunting task and, as the Editor, the final selection was mine.

The Poems chosen represent a cross-section of styles and content. They have been sent from all over the country, written by young and old alike united in the passion for writing poetry.

I trust this selection will delight and please the authors and all those who enjoy reading poetry.

Contents

The Power of Touch

Sparkling water, soft green grass,
velvet fur, slippery ice,
new born baby, silky hair,
shiny frog and silver sand,
the power of touch is in my hand.

Fevered brow, painful limb,
strength from one to one can flow,
illnesses and troubled minds,
hand on hand can mean so much,
how great the healing power of touch.

The warmth of love when someone dear
takes your hand, holds you close,
the power of touch I understand,
yet to explain I cannot start,
the unseen hand that touched my heart.

Andrea Pickup

A Mother's Love

There is a love that's like no other
It's that to children from their mother,
Fierce awesome nought can severe
In hell or heaven, nothing ever.

Should her children come to harm,
It doesn't take much to alarm,
Then like a tigress at bay,
Over her body none gains way.

Only let the person pause
Who would defy her deadly claws,
Hers is not to reason why,
With children lost she'd rather die.

Even a husband cannot part
Her children from her mother's heart,
So husbands try to understand,
If sometimes she seems out of hand.

It may be for her children's sake,
Should she at last the marriage break,
She suffers twice as much as you,
For her poor heart is torn in two.

If you can't or will not understand
You've failed your duty as her man,
Ashes to ashes dust to dust,
Bury her if spurn her you must.

If it takes the love light from your eye,
This love was merely born to die,
Flames lit vows made are all in vain,
For love once dead can't live again.

Lily Wallwork

A Silhouette of Pain

Shrouded by autumnal mist,
etched against the sky,
her face kissed by drops of rain,
she stood.
A silhouette of pain.
By a stream.
On a hill.
So silent, so still,
A vision? A ghost? A dream?
As if made of marble,
carved of stone or wood,
or so it would seem -
from the way she stood,
And time stood still,
Wrong!
A silhouette of pain,
made of flesh and blood,
kissed by mist and rain,
gave birth to song:
Why did you go away?
Without you I feel lost,
Why did you have to go
just when I love you most.

D Ryan

The Last Farewell

(For Apache and other old friends.)

Farewell my friend, it seems so sad
that you are old, and I am just a lad
Your pain is all I see in your eyes;
the decision hurts, but I know it's wise,
I love you too much too see you crippled, so
the vet says it's kinder to let you go
We'll meet again one day you and I;
but sadly now I must say goodbye.

Hazel Wilkinson-Wright

Father's Day

Father, father you're the best
I would never bother with the rest

And you have always looked after me
And you're so funny

You're the best dad
That other people wish they had

Oh I'm so glad for you
And for this day that only comes once a year

This very special day you see here
When I can say with a smile

Happy father's day
It's been worth while.

Paul Rogers (15)

The Lovely Elaine

I shall never forget the warmth of your soft hand, held
tightly in mine.
And I shall always remember that kiss, the one kiss you gave
me, a kiss so gentle, like mellowed wine.
For our worlds mingled that night, blended, as if in one,
and our hearts were free, free from pain.
I wish, how I wish, to hold your hand once more, my sweet,
sweet Elaine.

We talked nestled together, talked and talked, of cabbages
and of kings.
Talked of desires and delights, and many other wonderful
things.
Oh how we would walk with fingers laced, walk with rapture,
in the freshening rain.
If only, oh if only you were beside me, to walk together,
together forever, my lovely, lovely Elaine.

We sat, thoughts for each other, sipping our drinks, that
wondrous night we had, in that cosy little room.
There I hoped, sincerely hoped, that love would start to
bud, then burst with bloom.
Only now we are apart, loneliness tears my heart, and my
longing, longing for you, can never wane.
My thoughts of you, precious thoughts are ever with me, and
each night I miss you, my gentle, gentle Elaine.

Oft' I dream, dream of taking you, taking you tenderly, a
Summer's night, 'neath the velvet mantle of a jewelled sky,
gazing from above.
And my longing, aching longing deep within you, bestowing
you my seeds, seeds of lasting love.
Now I have a strength, a strength to determine, for your
love, I must strive to attain.
For tomorrow to touch, tomorrow to love, tomorrow to live,
my absent, absent Elaine.

Now you have left me, and wonder besets me, wondering where you are.
Thinking of what you are doing, of what you are dreaming, whilst from me, you are so afar.
So my love for you, ever will reach you, wherever you are, my darling Elaine.
For I know that someday, somewhere, somehow, we shall be together, forever, once again.

John Smyth

The Winds of Love

There are gentle puffs of breeze
Here on these little hills,
Reminding me with thrills
Of your brushed downy kisses.
The branches of the trees
Are bare in this autumn of my unhappiness
And the fallen leaves my tears.

I see in these branches your delicate tapering fingers
Spread across your face,
Your eyes peeping through,
Compassionate but with no love in them -
Only sorrow that you have hurt me.

You say there is no other
And if this be so please give me time,
All is not lost and I will woo
You again in the winter winds.

Higher now I climb
Where the wind is rough and gusty.
The loose stones and the buffeting
Render a precarious foothold,
But the summit at last is mine,
And with exhilaration I will descend running -
Knock boldly at your threshold
And, like the wind, sweep you off your feet,
And carry you away.
I cannot wait on another day.
Here down below the winter winds have gone,
And it is already Spring.

Harold R Middleton

Untitled

Then my pleasures were the earth and sky,
The snow peaks glowing pink in the dawn light,
The salty marshes and the wild ducks flight,
The peaty moorlands and the curlew's cry,
Snow flakes, rain's kisses and the soft winds sigh,
Good food and sleep, the silence of the night,
Colours, gardens, flowers, both scent and sight
Books music and the spells of poetry.
Stars light the earth at night and the moon's rays,
But when the sun has topped the eastern hill
You cannot see the stars shining above,
Although their feeble candles gutter still.
So now the starlight of my former days
Is lost amid the sunshine of our love.

Robert Everard Chadwick

The Ring

I could not sleep for this I know,
how I loved thee, yes I did,
I loved thee my darling, this day
through.
I loved thee always indeed I do,
Keepeth my love, keepeth my ring.

I watch each day passing for my love to
Return, but each goes and no-one comes
home,
If you need me my love, has I need
thee,
Keepeth my heart, keepeth my ring.

The sun doth shine on such a
wonderful day,
drenched in glorious sunshine, I am glad
God madeth this way.
I step back one day at a time, to hear
Your voice say, I do, one more time,
Keepeth my soul, keepeth my ring.

My love you no longer, breathe in God air,
and the life, we had together, no-one
Left to share,
To be with you my wife, all of my life,
In my heart, I can hardly wait,
I rushing my darling, to God's heavenly
Gate.
Keepeth my love, heart and soul, keepeth together
Keepeth our ring.

J Stott

Love Divine

Billowing, buffeting, vortexing snow
Smothering covering wherever it blows.
A maelstrom of white against the dark night
And a youngster alone to battle its might.

With faltering steps his heart full of fears
blinded with snow his eyes wet with tears
he bent his head to the fearful assault
and in his heart prayed he was not in default.

He trudged through the night, not a human in sight
to share with him this terrible plight
through ditches and fields, through woods and furrows
with many a tumble in rabbits' burrows.

Through his mind ran regrets and fears
shall he see again the isle of his birth
on whose shores the freedom he loved.
Perhaps now a dream of his childhood dove.

Oh why should we love to have taken away
the innocence of a child's love and play
to the end of his days this freedom he knew
would reincarnate each time to be new.

The pace and effort was taking its toll
the body was frozen and starting to fold
fourteen miles on that terrible night
was enough for this boy in his awful plight.

But beautiful and bright through his frozen mind
came a vision of the shepherd he loved as a child.
Then through his heart coursed the heat of his love
for a friend whom he knew loved him from above.

The boy survived this most terrible night
born by the love of the shepherd's might.

W Quenault

Tears and Laughter

When we smile, we smile
When we cry, there's tears
When we laugh, there's laughter
Laughter through the years
When we're gay, we're happy
When we're sad, there's gloom
Through the rain, comes rainbows
Beaming, in the noon
I love you, my darling
Though you're far, away
As I walk, I hear your voice
I dream of you, each day
My love, I write to you daily
I pour out, my heart
I hope, you'll soon be with me
Never more, to part
I just can't wait, to see you
I want you, oh, so much
My longing, drives me crazy
I just need, your touch
Now, I need to find you
I'll take a jet, or express train
My searching, straining, over
I'll be home, with you, again.

Helen M Hurley

Remember

Remember me remember do
The one who gave my all to you
And asked for nothing for my pain
Except to see your smile again
As lovers come and lovers go
Remember me who loved you so
My heart was broken on the day
You turned your back and walked away
For gold and wealth you traded me
But still my heart won't set me free
For all my suffering and my pain
I still would do it all again
Yes, I would swim the deepest sea
If on the shore you would wait for me
And dear, when you are old and grey
Your lovers all have turned away
When beauty's fading fast each day
Remember me and yesterday
And if you do, and call my name
You will find I love you just the same
The love you searched for far and wide
You will see is in my eyes.
As one by one friends come and go
Remember me who loved you so
The moon and stars bear witness to
The endless tears I've cried for you.
When wealth is dust. When truth is lies
I will kiss the tears from your dark eyes.

Pamela Harris

A Dream

I long to hold a babe in my arms,
One that is yours and mine,
Created by love
When we were as one
I wait and I wonder
When our time will be
When we can know the joy
of our own little baby.
Our love is true and strong
We laugh and love
Shout and cry just like people do -
And we'd love a baby too!
'I'm pregnant,' says my sister.
'Me too,' smiles a friend.
I'm happy for them and smile
Inside I cry and hope my heart will mend
I dream of a blonde-haired blue-eyed babe
Snuggled against me asleep,
Feeling so proud, I wipe a tear from my eye -
And hope my dream comes true.

Lynne Gavaghan

Untitled

I met her once at midnight,
But it seemed like the day,
We walked in the moonlight,
But the sun got in the way.

We kissed for the first time,
But I kissed her once before,
She danced in the east of nowhere,
But had never been there before.

So pretty in a red dress,
She told me it was blue,
In a veil of satin sunset,
This dream of mine is true.

We married on our fourth date,
She never wore my ring,
We made love in the Autumn,
She said it was in Spring.

She smiled in my presence,
And said I made her cry,
She never could ignore me,
But her shadow passed me by.

I've known her love forever,
But never met the girl before,
She said she'd never leave me,
But didn't want me any more.

We met in the moonlight,
She said it was midday,
I kissed her once at midnight,
But the sun got in the way.

Trevor Louis Wiggan

My Special Friend

When I came to Pelsall I left my friends behind
There was Beau and Fred and little Sam
Better friends were hard to find
We'd meet and have a doggy chat and then we'd go and play
When I said that I was leaving it really spoilt the day
When I left them all behind, I thought this is the end
When I get to Pelsall will I find a doggy friend?
I've walked across the common, looking left and right
I'd come back home all forlorn not a doggy friend in sight
Then one day I heard you, bark at Uncle Jim
When at last I saw you, you looked so smart and prim
I thought, 'She'll never play with me;' a pedigree so posh
I really ought to pop back in and get myself a wash
Come on I thought let's take a chance and try to have a game
I sidled up and said, 'Hello.' I didn't know your name
I heard that you were moving in, I thought at last a friend
I'll always love you Lucy right to the very end.

Joan York

A Poem by a Mature Student

I feel unusual, as if last night's kip didn't mean a lot,
It is now half-past one in the afternoon, more like one am.
And I have just come from the canteen, where I had lunch,
I had lunch with a girl who may or may not go out with me.

The young of today, or rather those people younger than I,
Are certainly stranger than I, for why, I have not discerned.
And I am not sure whether this girl will consider me as a mate,
Or, will she let me be, after a time of concern for me?

My head feels numb and 'dead' for some reason,
What a day to further persuade a girl to date,
What a day to describe to you, my computer friend,
With this head as it is, I'm glad I don't have to talk.

I had some lunch, as I have said, with an intent,
With the intention of clearing this unexplained fog
From between my ears; the brain that doesn't work.
But still I had lunch so that I could talk to her clearly.

It didn't work, my brain still doesn't work, a fog remains.
I could not describe this with the hindsight of tomorrow.
It would not be the same, it would be unreal, surreal.
But still I write, as if autornated, on autopilot, alone.

Ten thousand students, I have been told, come to college,
And yet I am still alone, I am not sure why this is so,
Or why this has happened, come to pass, come to be.
But nevertheless, I am alone, hungry for love.

Steven J Humphrey

The Shining Barrier

There is a Shining Barrier that nothing can penetrate,
Whatever is hurled against it - of cruelty, anger, hate;
Of spite, and malice, or malevolence, or evil at its worst,
Nothing has the power through The Barrier to burst.
All who dwell within this Shining Barrier are safe from all attack.
Whatever is thrown against them simply bounces back
And falls away, powerless to destroy, or to kill;
For The Shining Barrier shields completely from every kind of ill.

> Oft' times The Barrier is tested, and sore enemies assail,
> But *never,* for the one who *trusts,* does The Shining Barrier *ever* fail,
>
> For Love is the Shining Barrier - Love is that Impenetrable Shield.
> Love will *always* protect - Love will *never* yield.
> Love is *everlasting* - Love will *never* fade, or die.
> Love is an Impregnable Fortress in which to safely lie
> Secure within Its Shining Walls, wherein is Joy and Peace.
> Love is The Shining Barrier that grows to bring Release
> From all would be attacks of confusion, panic, doubt, or fear.
> With The Shining Barrier of Love around *nothing* evil can even draw near.

So let Love *abound* in its glorious Beauty - there for all to see . . .
- The Shining, Beautiful Barrier of Love surrounding you and me.

Esther Ruth King

Oh Please - Not Mine

Screaming rubber hits the ear,
Footsteps falter, people stare.
Windows open, heads appear;
Oh God - please not my baby.

Downcast eyes reflect the horror,
Murmured words express the sorrow.
He won't be three until tomorrow;
Oh God - please not my baby.

Oil and petrol in the mud,
Mingle with the pool of blood.
A too brief life nipped in the bud;
Oh God - please not my baby.

Golden curls now stained with red,
Twisted limbs and broken head,
Are they his and is he dead?
Oh God - please not my baby.

Clanging bells draw ever nearer,
Ambulance and stretcher bearer.
Soothing words and gentle carer;
Oh God - please not my baby.

Eyes closed tight and skin so white,
Pray that he will be alright.
The romper suit I bought last night;
Oh God - that is my baby.

Policeman taking notes specific,
Every detail realistic.
Tomorrow just one more statistic;
Oh God - please spare my baby.

E Wilson-Kembery

Feeling

Here I am in deepest thought,
In loneliness, I am distraught,
You in peace, content at last,
In all your pain, it now has passed,
I stood upon the moor alone,
I alone with thoughts of thee,
Then I felt a sense of peace,
Loving thoughts came over me,
You and I did tread this land,
In contentment hand in hand,
Thinking back when we were courting,
Watching stars when we were walking,
You said to me, 'We'll wed this year,'
Then every night, I'll love you dear,
I can still sense your kisses,
But now there is a sudden chill,
Sobbing for you nightly still.

Mayelf

Love you

I love you more than words can say
I love you more from day to day
You make my life each day so sweet
With you my life is so complete.

I love you more than Apple Pie
Peaches or fresh cream
You're the only one in my life
You're the only one in my dreams.

You've also said some hurtful things
I will remember 'til I die
The little things that hurt deep down
The things that make you cry.

But being in love is to forgive and forget
Or so the people say
I'll love you more forever and ever
I'll love you every day.

Carole Ann Wilkinson

My Baby

I used to want a baby,
With all my heart and soul,
And then one day, quite unexpectedly,
I found I was to reach my goal.
    For the father I had no feelings,
    Not in the way I should,
    So the baby was unwanted,
    I felt I'd have to get rid of it for good.
I never believed in abortion,
So that was immediately ruled out,
I'd have to have it adopted,
Of that there was no doubt.
    You may think I'm foolish,
    Or maybe just cold hearted,
    Though I assure you I'm not,
    I had to be this way, otherwise trouble would have started.
You see I couldn't love her properly,
I resented her too much,
Sometimes I'd sit and watch her,
But the baby, I couldn't touch.
    I knew eventually she'd have sensed it,
    And unhappy she would be,
    So why not give her up,
    And let her have a proper family?

Xanthe Story

A Kind of Love

You have a kind of love
that no one else can give,

A kind of love so big and strong
that we might forever live

You have love, so gentle
and yet so very strong.

A kind of love, that sees you through
when everything goes wrong

You have a kind of love
so gentle, and so very kind.

A kind of love, that sees you through
with a peace of mind.

You have love, that's everlasting
and so deep within

I want this love, so much
Where do I begin?

John Wilson

Kala

Beautiful child woman,
Your heart is bigger than you.
Don't let anyone ever tell you
That you're wrong to feel like you do.
Your honesty is refreshing,
Your compassion is divine,
I know that if I were the man you loved,
I'd be proud to have you as mine.
Your life as a woman has just started,
There's so much to see and do.
There's love to give
There's love to take,
With you it will always be true.
Your life is open, in front of you,
A book with pages bare.
What's written on those pages,
Depends on you, and
The people for whom you care.
Choose wisely little angel,
As sure as God's above,
Your life will be determined
By the people that you love.

S Andrassy

No Words Were Said

When I beheld that smile and form so rare,
And all the years before had never been,
There were no singers, but the songs were there
And you my love the fairest ever seen:
No words were said, how could this wonder be!
Your eyes they spoke the words I could not say,
And all the songs I knew, were there to see,
And though 'twas Winter, it was Spring that day.

Then when we walked that silent eve', and you
Outstretched your hand, no words I'd ever known
Could e'er compare that day, for then I knew
That words unsaid, were ours, and ours alone.
    No words were said, my dearest love, indeed
    For what are words, that we should ever need.

Alan R Stanley

Love

What is this thing called Love we cannot see,
We found it in a Mother's arms and sitting on her knee,

Then puppy love came and we were starry eyed,
Couldn't eat, or sleep it held us in a trap,

We think our hearts would break the excitement too much to bare,
When true love comes at last we float on air.

Working hard no time to spare we took it for granted and then one
day it wasn't there,

Why didn't we tender it like a delicate flower,
Nurture it touch it, caress it and care,

Love is a mystery it can't be bought or sold,
It comes from within from the Heart and Soul,

If it finds us worthy it will take hold,
Its wonder is a Miracle we all Behold,

So if you find it don't laugh or scorn,
Because if you've never tasted it, you wish you had never been
born.

You're like a ship without an anchor tossing in the Storm.
But Love holds us steady makes us Strong and True,

It shows in our eyes and gives off a Glow that only True
Love can Bestow.

Avril Fedoryszyn

So Near my Heart

My dearly beloved, mine
own heart's desire,
Tell me you love me, set
me afire,
Afire with touch of
your kisses, so sweet
Afire with embraces,
to make my heart beat,
A beat with the thought
you ever here,
Astir with knowing
you ever near,
Yet how to finish
this,
I don't know quite,
For 'Darling', I think
of you, by day and
by night,
So 'Dear one', think
of me while we are apart.
For you are the one
'So near my heart'.

Denys George Hill

Do you Care

Do you care, what others feel, as you travel
on your way, do you give a cheery smile, and
pass the time of day, or do you briskly pass
them by, looking left nor right, but ogle all
the pretty girls, that pass within your sight.

Fate is fickle, and unfair, never gives an even
share, of life's good things, to those in sorrow
or deep despair, so stop a moment, and say, how are
you, how is the world treating you, you'll see the
hope, shine in their eyes, that someone cared to
recognise, a word of cheer is their need, they will
certainly appreciate your thoughtful deed.

So let's resolve to brighten each day, with a cheerful
word, as we are on our way, the world will
seem a better place, with a cheerful word and smiling
face, let's see the kindness, dry the tears, drive away
the doubts and fears, life's too short, to worry each
day, and year, away.

John Toms

The Black Knight

(For cousin Robert off to war).

Of swarthy skin, and flashing eye,
With spirit proud and free,
He's one of those who'd do or die
For such as you and me.

And yet his heart is warm and kind,
And not immune from love,
A sort of love you seldom find
(not cooing like a dove),
but standing like a bulwark,
to protect and comfort all
Who hold a little cranny
Inside his heart's strong wall.

He calls himself *the Black Knight*
And yet to me it seems
He is the whitest of them all,
This man who acts, not dreams.

M Morton

Dubai

As I sit her calm and free
Watching the waves dance over the sea
Seeing the birds flying high in the sky
I really know I'm in Dubai.

The golden sands, the palm trees green
And lots of camels around to be seen
I'll gasp and wonder and I'll sigh
I really know I'm in Dubai.

Around the souke I stand and gaze
The stalls, the fruit in a colourful blaze
And all those spices my oh my
I really know I'm in Dubai.

The places built with lavish splendour
And the people proud but tender
Here I'll sleep and here I'll lie
I really know I'm in Dubai.

The mosques stand tall and oh so grand
They add more beauty to this land
And I would hate to say goodbye
As I really know and love Dubai.

Samantha Hammond

The Love of Mary and Joseph

Love that distance cannot erase
Time cannot separate,
Love born from whence time began
Blossoming in a desert place.
Magnetism in human form
The need to touch unheeded,
Man in his carnality
Can only disbelieve it.

Why is it unbelievable?
do we need eyes to see?
Bees can pollinate the flowers
God can join the he's and she's.
A miracle born of perfection
Two unite to make a whole,
Joined in mutual adoration
Man and woman, girl and boy.

Christine Parker

For I am a Woman

I am a woman
I feel and I see
I need to be touched
To be loved
Yet somehow the magic once held around me
Has faded away into dust

The pain in my heart will not go away
The fear of rejection seems firmly to stay
The loss of my lover my friend my life
Has left me so empty
Not even a wife

No more am I young with the sparkle I had
Just growing older lonely and sad
Is this all that's left for me
Through the rest of my life
No more kisses or rainbows
No more trouble and strife

I am a woman I feel I see
Please open your eyes
Look now look at me.

Margaret Elliot Woods

Messages of Love

When the Good Lord beckons a loved one to enter
His beautiful domain
To exist in eternal happiness, free from all suffering
and pain
Don't think your loved one has left you because that
isn't true
They have only passed over to the other side,
something we eventually all do.
Try not to spend your time grieving, it's not what
they want from you
Or encircle yourself with pity, until depression
obscures your view.
Instead, try conversing with your loved one - the
effort will not be in vain.
Although they're not there in person, their spirit is
there just the same.
Then look for those little messages, like the warmth
in the Winter's sun
Or the flower that blooms extra early, all are a
message of love.
And many many more, too numerous to mention,
which you can recognise if you heed and pay
attention.
So try not to spend your time grieving, or let
depression obscure your view.
Instead, keep watch for those messages, sent with
love especially for you.

Jean Breach

The Land I Love

How sweet is Wales the land of song
How sweet is this place where I belong
Well I tell you the truth from a Welshman's heart
It's the land I love, the land of art
With beautiful hills and grass of green
The darkest woods I have ever seen
Where a cloud of pride fills the air
With miners' valleys, beyond compare
The national language is often *spoke*
As I listen to tales from the elderly folk
The anthem sung is full of glory
The rugby field is another story
The rivers run from their mountain springs
The warmth from the church as the choir sings
This wonderful land was made with thought,
A lesson from God, which I have been taught.

Greg Ebenezer

National Smiling Week

When your life is one bed of sweet roses
And you sail on the crest of a wave,
It's so easy to smile and be happy
Far too easy to jeer at the grave.

It's natural to smile at loved ones who care
Who'll return them, your favour to win,
Naturally, smile at your daughter or son
This will rapidly spread to a grin.

It's usual to smile with neighbours and friends
And it's usual to laugh at a pun,
Plenty of gravy - luck of the Navy
Then life's highway is mirrors of fun.

It's heaven to smile with your baby love
And it's gracious to smile for the Queen,
When lovers are locked in a *firework's embrace*
Well, you've giggled at this saucy scene!

Smile at your dog who'll respond in a flash
He's expecting some bones or a walk,
At cocktail affairs, just smile at the stares
For they mix well with dry sherry talk.

So, dear brothers and maidens *Keep Smiling*
For the Nation requires this from you,
Should you wilt from the weight of your taxes
Well, keep smiling - I'm overtaxed too!

For smiles are like wine - and yours are divine!
But I've thought about this thing for years,
The loveliest smile, the one to beguile
Is the smile that can break through the tears!

G Shales Hind

My Mother

There was a woman that I loved
much more than any other.
She carried me for nine long months
of course she was my Mother.
Well under five feet tall she stood
and weighed a mere six stone.
But on that day she passed away
I was left alone.
Many times after she'd gone
I'd walk to her gate,
because I needed her so much
of course it was too late.
I wanted to apologise
for giving her such worry,
to cuddle her and say oh Mum
I'm really very sorry.
She wasn't old just fifty four
when she passed away.
I still see her lying there,
like it was yesterday.
She'd had trouble with her heart
and suffered from Angina.
Now she is suffering no more
my Mother, none was finer.
Many years have passed since then
but not a single day
do I not sit and think of her
and wonder what I'd say.
If only for a minute she
could walk in my front door,
I'd say I love you Mother dear
always and evermore.

David Wilson .

The Scotsgirl and the Red Indian

There was this Scotsgirl worked in Edinburgh,
She'd saved up all her pay,
To travel abroad to Canada,
For a two week holiday.

There she met up with this Red Indian,
He was an awesome sight,
With his axe and feathered head,
She thought, he looks a bit of alright!

His hands they were like shovels,
Like tree trunks were his thighs,
He stood up like a mountain,
Six foot six between the eyes.

She called him Big Chief Jimmy,
He called her Tartan Dove,
And by the end of the two weeks,
They were both in love.

Then said the Scotsgirl to her Indian,
'Tell me - will you marry me true?'
He answered, 'Yes! and if we have a baby,
We can call it Hawk-eye the Noo!'

Kevin Fitzgerald

Leaving

(For Lorna M)

I wake every morning to find you're not there,
I reach out to touch you and the bed is bare,
And being all alone is driving me mad,
My heart aches for you and the pain is so bad.

Just left me all alone without saying a word;
You walked out the door, thoughts and feelings left unheard,
With no chance to talk, you made no attempt to explain,
That's the reason now that I am in such pain.

I pray that in the years to come,
You'll think of me and what you have done,
But whatever, my life will go on with me smiling through,
For I've not lost out, because the loser is you.

D Allen Stevenson

A Mother's Love

I love my kids
with all my heart
To stay close
and never part
To help them
if in trouble
I would be there
on the double
I would try
to understand
And always lend
a helping hand
To give them something
I never had
which makes me
feel very sad
A mother's love
I wish I had

Mary Rose Wilson

Amputee

He lay between the sheets, two beds from mine,
We all knew that he'd stepped on a Jerry mine.
Had lost his right foot just below the knee,
But that wasn't all - he'd lost his private three.

So badly mangled - surgeon had to amputate.
Said from life that he would like to abdicate.
Two letters from his girlfriend unopenec by his bed,
Said he wished he'd sprung the AP with his head.

Not the dead who pay the highest price in war,
But severe amputees who'll suffer fifty years or more.
Padre knelt and said a prayer to beloved God above.
Did he ask why he'd deprived our warrior of love?

Harry F Eaton

Shannon

Dear little Shannon
Sent for us to love,
A precious little gift
For us to cherish and to love.

Your life was like a season
A quarter of a year,
Our sunshine and our summer
A life we held so dear.

What it felt to love you
Only we will ever know,
A part of us died
The day you had to go.

I only held you for a little while,
But in that time I knew
That in the years to come
I'd share a bond with you.

I think about you every day
And what might have been,
But what happened
Was something unforeseen.

You're with your nan and grandad
Looking down from up above
Dear little Shannon
Who was sent for us to love.

Mary Wood

Happy Birthdays

Once I had a baby
She's not that anymore,
There's Sindy and there's Barbie
and there's lego on the floor!
She's growing up and up now
Why! - In June she'll be *four.*

Twice I had a baby
She was born too soon
You see she died
Alone in my womb,
But she was *life* in me
and in August she'll be *three.*

Three times I had a baby
A son to carry on the name
But please don't forget him
'cos into *our lives* he came
After thirty-two hours he was gone
and in March he will be 'one'.

Three special little people
Loved so very much,
In many ways all still alive
But only one to touch

But each and every year
We're happy don't you see
We're left with *Happy Birthdays*
- One, two, three.

Sue Chambers

Life's Road

Life's road is full of ups and downs
Happiness pain and strife,
This is what makes up our destiny
As we enter into life,
Our paths are all mapped out for us
What is to be will be,
This I believe to be true
That we grow just like a tree,
Its roots are where we come from
Its bark our body strong,
Its branches are the roads we take
As life just leads us on,
The fruit it bares is the food we eat
Its leaves cover to keep us warm,
Its branches form a canopy
To protect us from life's storm,
And as the seasons come and go
And life slips quickly by,
I like to think that none of us
Don't ever really die,
But just pass on to a better place
Where there's no suffering and no pain,
And our loved ones who have gone before
We shall meet them all again.

Muriel Cooper

Untitled

Children growing, caring, showing
Love for Mum and Dad.
Walking, riding, talking sleeping
Doing nothing bad.

Then one day temptation strikes
Try sniffing this they say.
Children growing, caring showing
But with their lives they pay.

Hiding from the ones who love them
Looking, feeling bad.
Wish they'd listened to their friends
Especially Mum and Dad.

But alas too late they listen
As pals and friends feel ill.
Can they survive and realise
Drugs are a bitter pill.

Better now I guess I'm lucky
I took advice when given.
Back at home with Mum and Dad
Lucky to be forgiven.

Sue Grice

Destination Unknown

From being a pup I've stayed by your side
I always thought that you owned me with pride
I've been a good dog and I've done my best
But now you've put me to the test
A test of faithfulness, one wonders
If so, I should have passed with honours
Thrown out of a car in a dirty back street
Without explanation, water or meat

It's now two days later and as you can see
I'm still waiting for you to come back for me
As a car approaches I think you've returned
My love for you no longer spurned
The joy I feel one cannot measure
I wag my tail in frenzied pleasure
With new-found energy now I bound
Towards that old familiar sound

Accepting the punishment you've put me through
I'm always forgiving and still I love you
You've been away from me so long
And I'm truly sorry if I've done wrong
But the car doesn't stop and there's no reprieve
Again, I'm left all alone to grieve
I yearn so much for your protection
But now my head droops in true dejection

A lady arrives and strokes my head
Kindly she speaks, then away I'm led
Into a van, but I still feel alone
As I travel along, destination unknown
I arrive at a dog pound somewhere, somehow
But I'm even more unhappy now
I'm being fed and I'm warm and dry
But if I were human I would cry

My kennel here is a lonely place
And I long for the sight of a familiar face
Yet still the sound of your voice I hear
And feel that you must be somewhere near
As day after day I listen and wait
While your return I anticipate
I always thought that I understood you
You surely wouldn't abandon me - would you?

A Shears

Our Ben

We loved our happy little dog,
For over fourteen years
But sad to say, he's gone away
Our eyes are filled with tears

Wherever we went, he came along
We never, ever left him.
He'd sit up straight, and view
the scene
Although his sight was dim.

He loved to snuggle, close to me.
And how he loved a treat.
He wasn't fond, of doggie food,
But loved some chicken meat

He lost one eye, a while ago
It never did deter him.
But now and then, he stumbled
His eyes were getting dim

But, sad to say, soon came the day
We knew his sight had gone
The vet advised, the time had come
We never brought him home.

Nora Nelson

Can This be Heaven

A garden with a golden gate
will open as you enter it
A choir of angels standing round
and heavenly music is the sound
In the midst you see a face
so kind so good so full of grace
He welcomes you with open arms
Now you're at peace no one can harm.

The garden full of many flowers
Grass so green without the showers
Sky deep blue like our Lord's eyes
Now I'm sure I'm in paradise
He speaks to me with loving words
Our God, Holy Jesus, Christ
No more death for you,
Just everlasting life.

M Ball

Waiting; The Right Time

As my head turned in the dismal street,
I knew at once that we would meet,
I'd roamed around for all my life,
Looking, searching, but all in strife.

I seemed to have searched everywhere,
Beginning to think that no one cared,
And after my life has come and gone,
My love for you would still be strong.

In the dark city of the age old past,
Was it a feeling that would never last?
I'd lost love but gained a friend,
A friendship that would never end.

And in the heavens I would wait,
Standing beside the Golden Gate,
You'd arrive, I'd take your hand
And together we'd walk to the
Promised Land.

Vanessa Grof

Helping Others

As you go through life
Give a helping hand
To those who walk beside you
Who may not understand.

Give a cheery smile
To those along the way,
Some may be in need
Or have a bad day.

Helping other people
Is what we're here to do,
To try to lift a burden
And help a person through.

Then as you help others
You will find it's true,
What you do to others
Will come back to you.

Jean M Webster

The Lancashire Lady

Far out in the distance,
her lonely figure strolls,
shimmering through the hazy light,
she is lost among the falling snow.

I long to see your face again,
look into your warm and grateful eyes,
to see the light of love within,
again glow and sparkle into our lives.

The figure I see dances with joy,
a young body full of strength and agility,
it is now free of all pain and suffering,
free of all the aged fragility.

I call for you, please don't leave again,
and I despair as the distance grows,
I call for you, please don't leave again,
but you slowly slip away.

As time goes by the pain will not die,
and it lays like lead upon my heart,
you left before I could say goodbye,
and that sad memory still haunts me.

Far out in the distance,
your lonely figure strolls,
but your existence is just a shady dream,
deep within my mourning mind.

I long to hear your voice again,
to listen to your wise old words,
to let me know your love still lives,
and help me quell my endless tears.

Bridget T Hellewell

Memorable

You walked into my life,
and things that fell apart,
all seemed to mend so quickly,
by the kindness in your heart,
I wanted to be with you,
be with you night and day,
what is it that you've got,
that makes me feel this way,
and now this poem's ending,
my memories never fade,
I'll look back some years later,
to see the mark you've made.

Allison Hughes

The Longed for Love

With you my darling I found the love
I longed for.
The look of love in yours tells all
I feel the love when we touch each other.
I can sense the love in the way you
take care of me.
For myself there will be no other
love in my life time.
The way you buy me flowers says
it all.
The way you kiss me gentle and
warm lets me know that you love me.
In the way that you hold me tight as
we dance together shows that we belong
together.
I know you love me because best of
all you tell me that you love me with all
of your heart and soul.

Tracey Forsyth

If Only

Like a flower that grows
My love shows
It blossoms every day.
Like a bird that flies
My love thrives
From the little things you say.
Like a dream come true
Of me and you
Together 'til the end.
Like you wanting me
As I want you
And not only as a friend.

Diane Duxbury

Untitled

A really good marriage is like a good book.
Chapter one is the marital vow that you took
As the story goes on it takes many turns
And from each page I know each of us learns
Some parts do get boring, we lay the book
down
And pick it up later when a smile takes the
frown
It isn't all happy, but without the sad
We wouldn't know joy or how to be glad
the story line gets more exciting each day
But without one another you'd not find the way.
You'd soon lose your page in this wonderful tale
If you think part way through that things have
gone stale.
So read on together, there's goods bits all through
Just give to each other, whatever you do.
You reach chapter forty, halfway to the end,
When you've finished the story, please give
me a lend!

Marilyn Gunther

A Fairy Wedding

I heard the tinkling of a bell, its ring was clear and sweet,
It was the tinkling of a bell upon a fairy's feet,
I stood behind the nearest bush as down the glade she came with a rush:
What is her hurry? Where does she go?
I'll follow quietly, then I will know:

Very soon I saw a sight, I rubbed my eyes, could this be right?
Dozens of fairies, goblins and gnomes
Dancing around their tiny homes, and in the middle of that fairy ring
Upon this throne sat a fairy king,
His tiny chest was filled with pride, a beautiful fairy sat by his side.

Ah! Now it was plain for me to see,
The fairy I saw was his bride-to-be:
Goblin courtiers in velvet blue, pixie footmen in scarlet hue,
Firefly horses, gold crested coaches,
Lords and their ladies, with sapphire brooches:

And all around this tiny glade the colours of the rainbow
Were being displayed.
As all the guests danced to and fro,
Alas it is time for me to go:
With lagging steps, but a happy heart, this secret glade I must depart.

Brian Ducker

Love is a Guest

No more fishing in old wounds my love
Trade that bait for gold my love
It's time to throw anchor my love
The sea isn't buckling now my love
Bring those limbs to new life my love
It's time to dry the soul my love
And walk the spirit naked my love
No more raping the rose my love
Jealousy isn't green now my love
And love is over the ocean rise my love
Don't worry about the planet my love
Man is but a time bomb ticking my love
God is out of his time my love
Blood moves the hand my love
Politics is never a still pool my love
But the shadow always parts my love
So sink your eyes in rest my love
For Love is a guest my love
Love is a host my love
Treat the guest well my love
If you wish to host the heart my love.

Collin Rossini

The Gift

I gave you a present,
With eyes shining,
Arms outstretched.
You received it with alacrity
And with greedy fingers
Began to unwrap it.
You pulled the gift to pieces,
Scorn in your voice,
A sneer on your face,
Threw down the remains
At my feet
And walked away,
Not recognising the value.
My heart shrivelled, for
The gift I had given you was -
All my love.

M Finchett

Addiction

You seemed to be the person
to make the hurting end,
someone I could lean on
a truly loyal friend

When friends we changed to lovers
I could have reached the skies,
but how was I to know
about the deceit and lies

You had another love
this type beyond compare,
I couldn't win you from her
the hold was already there

Slowly I began to learn
you needed her more than me,
the rings around your eyes
the screaming in your sleep

I tried to get you help my love
to stop the growing pain,
but this one was too strong my love
and would win you once again

The drugs replaced our love
she wanted all of you,
you couldn't handle life with me
or me life with you

Andrea A Felix

Love Song

The quiver of an arrow as it flies straight from
its bow.
The murder of a gentle stream, quiescent in
its flow.
The trilling of a tiny lark way high upon
the wing.
Are reminiscent of her voice when she
begins to sing.

The arrow gains momentum as it speeds
towards its goal.
The stream's soft murmur deepens as it broadens
in its bowl
The larks faint trill makes music as to earth
it gently flies
And confidence lend volume to the voice I
idolise.

Her song plays like a Zephyr upon my
pounding heart
And gently soothes the aching I thought would
ne'er depart.
Leaving sweet contentment and love so
long desired.
Her hand in mine, fulfilment of the
dream her song inspired.

Winifred Thomas

Eternal Rose

A rose lay down one stormy day,
its petals spread about.
The fragrance of the rose now gone,
its life now flickered out.

Yet from this rose there fell a seed,
new life to take its place.
To grow up where the rose had died,
to fill the empty space.

I too once knew of such a rose
with fragrance good and true.
But like the storm God took her from me
and left me to see life through.

All alone, not knowing where to turn,
heartbroke without a friend.
Wishing deep down it was I who'd gone,
hoping to meet my end.

Then all at once my whole life changed
for suddenly there was you.
The seed who'd come to fill the space
and start my life anew.

If like that rose our love grows tall
and blossoms to a high.
Then we too shall share eternal love
and no more shall the roses die.

Leonard Dronsfield

The End of the Sun for the One I Loved

Moments are losing themselves, like wind in the trees,
And there are moments I'm looking for
Like those I lost when my lips fell to yours.

In the lap of reality, myths are regenerating,
His face gets brighter and heavier.
His ancestral body appears slowly
And the tired days collapse.

Alone, I'm screaming, it's dust in the wind,
Because he just died again.
Stars were his love's dreams, blood in his thoughts,
He wanted to run in the dark caves
To walk on improvised soil.

He trusted in a fictive sky, he believed that a true
Love is still, but the silence was there.
He wanted to run on his own road,
To reach the silence of the lies,
To feed the soul, which was drying in him
He wanted to run into the moonless night.

To leave this world, to walk on the road where he would
Be loved, where he could hold somebody's hand.
A winter's night, he let his dreams
Go free from his throat, the blades in a glimpse
Of mortal power, finished the last gasp.
I cry, wounded because I didn't understand
The end of the sun for the one I loved.

Since that night, Winters are like the darkest stars
And the silence is there.

Nina-Ann Lewis

The Ship of Life

You're eyes are like an ocean,
Blue, calm and deep,
Sometimes I look into that ocean,
When I lay down to go to sleep,

Upon this travels *our* ship,
Floating through the sea,
Sometimes rocked by vicious storms;
Which settle back to tranquillity,

Why does this ship not sink?
It seems to always stay afloat,
It's because the two-people-on-board
Believe in love, faith and hope,

Deep, deep down below the surface,
There are ships that have been forgotten,
Overwhelmed in tidal waves of anger,
Left to sink, erode and go rotten,

Did anyone notice them go?
Did anyone really care,
Now they sit in the memory,
Of someone who knows they are there,

Some ships are built for battle,
Some ships are built for fun,
Others are built for cruising,
But *ours* has all these in-one!

There is a moral to this poem;
Nothing moves smoothly all the way,
Sometimes there can be difficult times,
With love and faith, it helps us to try, and
understand, and stay.

S Barrasso

Untitled

Love knows no age
No limit of time
No conditions -
Love is sublime -

Imagine how great
the love of the one
Who created the World
Since time begun

A love never endless
A love never tired
Through all mans' mistakes
Loves' forgiveness . . . transpired

How can that compare
With the love of a Man
Our capacity for love
Has a limited span -

Little things niggle
And get in the way
And a perfect love
Can be lost in a day -

If our God was that hard
With our own small mistakes
We would be . . . no more
The World's heart to break!

Barbara Weymount

I Can't

I'd like to say I love you
But honestly, I can't
I'd like to hold you in my arms
and cherish you, I can't.
I'd like to love and touch you
caress you too, I can't.
I'd like to press my lips to yours.
A lasting kiss, but can't.
I'd like to hold your hand in mine
and clasp it tight but can't.
I'd like to whisper in your ear
words of love, but can't.
I'd like to pet and comfort you
look after you, but can't.
I'd like to say I love you
but honestly, I can't.

James Hope-Knutsford

Ideals

People talk about loving;
But I can't understand,
That all the love in the world,
Is never close at hand.

People talk of peace,
Now that could never be;
Until the world could work and live
In perfect unity.

People talk of truth,
But that will never be known,
Until the world realises it's time,
The seeds of truth were sown.

People all have ideals,
This is how it should be,
That love, peace and truth,
Should combine in harmony.

W T Crowther

My Wife

She understands my ups and downs
All my laughters all my frowns
To love and cherish was her vows
God only knows how she's kept those vows
Her love and devotion I much admire
My love for her will never tire
Raised her family with love and care
Comforted them when in despair
Seen them through the trials of life
I bless the day I met my wife
Time has passed we're still together
My love for her will last forever.

R Chadwick

Battle for Love

Love is a blind alley.
No doors to escape,
No windows to view.
A single thought
A reflection of you.
All dangers exist,
But non are sought.

The heart is melting,
The mind becomes numb.
Unknown passions burn within.
I dig the trench around my heart,
The battle begins,
A fight for truth.

I become another victim,
A casualty of love.
The soul is weak,
It falls to the force,
The force of true love.
A blinding white light,
Of a passion so true.

Love is a blind alley,
No doors to escape,
No windows to view.
My heart,
My soul,
My love,
Belongs to you.

H Dann

Richness of Love

There will be no other like you
No one could take your place
but we will always have our
memories, to cherish and embrace,
We will always have the love
you gave without reserve,
Your common sense and wisdom,
Your warmth, your strength,
your nerve.
Material things you didn't have
Yet! you were the richest man
on Earth, your riches were your
family, multiplied with each
new birth.
So close your eyes and rest
now, you gave the best you had,
We'll be here for one another
We love you, *Thankyou Dad.*

Pauline Fogerty

The Seed of Love

(Dedicated to Tony with love 'From me to you'.)

We planted the seed giving
it life
the man I loved then made
me his wife
We shared the good times
and the bad
We shared the happy and
the sad
The heartaches came as they
often do
We stood united and saw
them through
Pulling together come
what may
We'd smile as we made it
through another day
The seed of love is planted
deep
There to flourish and to
keep
It may start to wither and
die
Then the time has come to
say goodbye
We tried so hard to hang
on in there
But life's pressures proved
too hard to bear
Some seeds by the wayside
fall
It's really no one's fault at
all
The marriage breaks down
it falls apart

All that remains is a
broken heart.
I thought we'd stand the
test of time
After twenty four years it's
simply a crime
Can't live with you can't
live without
Forever my first love of that
there's no doubt
Seeds can be replanted to
start anew
Perhaps one day that's what
we'll do
Two hearts mending challenging
all fears
Forgetting the past in our
twilight years

Carol Anne Burnup

Proposal

Beloved heart,
Cede this my plot tomorrow's smile.
As sundered wings we'd join and part
Immortal aires to weave awhile.

C Finnegan

Love

Love is a precious thing,
It seems to last forever,
But when it turns to go away,
Your heart breaks and you think you'll never
love again,
. . . Ever!

Elizabeth Anne Jessup

September 14th 1991

Today is such a special day,
My grandaughter Sharon was given away.
I'm sure everyone thinks she's a beautiful bride,
Especially Mark who stands by her side.

From the day she was born, she's been loved so dearly,
By her Mum and Dad and brothers sincerely.
But Grans and Grandads played a small part,
They also loved her from the start.

With so much love, she has plenty to give,
And I know that she will, as long as she lives.
So let them look forward to many happy years,
With plenty of sunshine; and not many tears.

We wish them lots of sunshine,
But we know they'll need the rain.
As long as they keep on loving,
Their happiness will remain.

So may they be blessed on this happy day,
As they travel along their new pathway.
Hand in hand, always together,
Facing each day, whatever the weather.

With lots of love from Grandad and Nan . . .

Ida Cunningham

My Belovéd

Without your love I could not go on.
I need your strong arm to lean upon.
When days are dark, and nights seem drear.
I always want you to be near.

We've been together a long time now.
And there's many more lines upon your brow,
But in my heart is the memory still,
When we made our vows and said 'I will.'

The fiery passion has died away,
But in its place has come to stay
A quiet serenity, that will be
A haven of rest for you and me.

Lady Sarah

Eternal Love

You came to me one day in Spring
Not so long ago,
I still can hear the cuckoo sing
And see the April snow,
We loved each other from the start
That love will never die,
We need each other even more
As each day passes by,
You are the very air I breathe,
The sun that shines so bright,
Your eyes are like the little stars
Twinkling in the night,
When everywhere is dark and cold
Your laughter keeps me warm,
You made my life complete, dear Son
The day that you were born.

Paula Jacobs

First Love

Do you remember your first love, like me? -
Do you remember the feeling of glee -
Heart fluttering, lips smiling, eyes all aglow,
Do you remember how you loved him so?

How did you come to go separate ways,
Was it because of your growing up phase?

Does he still hold a love in the corner of your heart?
And, like me, have you cherished this love from the start? -

Do you wonder where he is?
And does he think of you?
Yes, you'll remember your first love,
like me,
all life through!

Joan Carr-Lancashire

Beloved

He told me that he loved me - with a twinkle
in his eye. He said that he would love me
'til the sun fell from the sky. He held
my hand and kissed me, laid his head
upon my breast. His head grew heavy,
hand relaxed, he slept in tranquil rest.

We stretched out there, half-dreaming, quite happy
and content - I brushed his wavy hair
and thought of what to me, he meant:
and whispered, 'God, I thank you that he
is truly mine. This love of ours is surely
something glorious and divine.'

He stirred, I said, 'Hush, hush, my
dear, please rest a little while.'
His sleepy eyes then opened and he
gave me such a smile. He
reached across and touched my
face and I felt so alive. It's
wonderful to have a son who'll
soon be all of five!

Amelia Howarth

When did Love go out of Fashion?

When did love go out of fashion?
I don't mean sex and lust,
I mean that deep emotion from which, springs
caring, peace and trust.
When love went out of fashion, was I not even born?
I thank God I was given to a family who, still knew
and practised this the greatest, of art forms.
Why did love go out of fashion and people stop being
there?
Love wild free and good for all who have a care,
Bring love back into fashion by practising in your
lives,
A little *love thy neighbour*,
Go on flash them your great gorgeous smile.
I don't care about fashion let it explode itself,
For love is still for me the most important element,
towards keeping my good health.

Gemma Alexander

Immortal Love?

When poets tell us of their love they say
That it will last forever, come what may.
When future generations read their verse,
They say their love lives on, beyond death's curse.

But words of love and romance testify
Not to the fact their love could never die,
But to the real intensity of feeling
Which for a little while had sent them reeling.

Their heartfelt words can move us down the years.
Their love brought back to life brings us to tears.
But later poems might show that love can fail,
And tell us of a new love or betrayal.

For though a moderate love can surely last,
The passion they describe will burn out fast.
So if you seek some pure, eternal flame,
It is love's *poem* that wins immortal fame.

Phil Webster

The Golden Age

And you, my love, I should not leave behind.
Take my hand, merge your soul with mine.
Let us take a trip together
Flying through the changing weather.

Fear not the unknown: The light will guide us
Drawing from the flame inside us.
Passing through the six dark ages
Looking down on granite pages.

And when we are in the cusp of seven
Breathe awhile for this is Heaven.
Meet your God who lives on Zion
Sun and moon above the lion

For when oceans burst and land is torn
A new Atlantis will be born.
Sign your name on the Good Book's page.
Please join me in the Golden Age.

Jennifer Emms

Love's Uncertainty

I feel inside of me a fear
I feel the end of Paradise is near
And yet, for all that, and heaven too
I won't outlive the memory of you.
Strange exotic being that you are
Make me neglect my tasks and dream afar
Of Shangri-La, where just we two could hide
And leave all miserable uncertainties outside,
To live as God and we would will, to recreate
To reproduce ourselves with love that knows its mate
And yet - inside of me a fear
I feel the end of Paradise is near
Of much exciting beauty that was mine
And all of me, heart, soul and thought was thine
To conjure with, and play, with jealous hate
Which feared that others may also share my fate
But no! This cannot be mine, this morbic thought
You can't forget - and yet in vain I seek
To quell inside of me a fear
A fear the end of Paradise is near.

Muriel Barlow

Emotions - Love

This word love - what does it mean?
Is it for real - perhaps it's a dream.
I love to sing, I love to shout.
This thing love, what is it about?
Where does love start and where does it end?
Who do you love - your family, your friends?
And when you're in love, how will it show?
Will someone tell you, or will you just know?
Love can be happy, and sometimes sad.
Love can be good, but sometimes bad.
Love can be cruel, it can also be kind
Can love see, or is love blind?
To me love is all of these things,
and a million more,
Because love began, when the world began,
and will go on forever more.

Kim Thorne

The Lovers' Prayer

Oh! Heavenly Father up above,
Please protect the one I love.
Keep her safe and always sound,
No matter where she may be bound.
Let her know and let her see,
That as I love her may she love me.
Amen.

Michael Leslie Burnell

Love

In Devonshire we have a word,
Four-letter word,
Which foreigners are much bemused,
Nay, not amused,
To hear.

Soft voices of the West Country
My West Country,
So call both visitor and friend
And don't intend
To mock.

How heart-warming, then, to return,
'Tis to return
To Devonshire, to hear again
In sweet refrain,
This word.

Four-letter words are known to be -
Yes, known to be -
Both coarse and rude, best left unsaid;
Nor ever read
Aloud.

But Devon men say easily,
So easily,
This word they heard in cradle days.
With them it stays
Always.

Don't look at me with doubting eyes,
Sad, doubting eyes.
You mean to tell me you've not heard
This lovely word,
Love? *Love.*

Joan Head

What is Love?

What is love I ask the Lord
above?
Love is life, love is love.
Why oh why can I not
find love.

Please oh Lord help me
find love.
I have learnt to give it
with your help.
Please oh Lord help me
reach out.

Reach out to the ones
I love most.
Reach out so I can hold
them close.
This is love from the Lord
above.
Love is for all, love is to
be loved.

C Matthews

Untitled

When love dies,
all winds blow cold.
No saving grace from any Summer breeze,
can shield the heart from such as these.
When love dies.

When love dies,
all joy is gone.
Each raindrop that once seemed, a happy tear,
falls from dark skies, that once were clear.
When love dies.

When love dies,
all colour fades.
Where every blossom once, had shed its own sweet light,
now shadows fold and put the sun to flight.
When love dies.

When love dies,
all comfort, pain.
Though time that heals creeps on, still breath to breath,
the lover dies a little death.
All else is lies,
When love dies.

G W Murphy

Love Story

Forget me not if I should die
Remember our life together.
And how we walked over mountains green
Through the wild fern and the heather.
Think of me as time goes on
Of happy days spent with each other.
As we strolled along and spoke of love
Our thoughts were for each other.
Forget me not if I should die
Our love will live forever.
We always vowed should this be so
It was something no one would sever.
The years will roll on but our love won't die
Memories will remain in their glory
Because our love was strong
And we became one
And we have this beautiful love story.

Marie Hodges

Love

Oh how I sing in happy measure of countless hours spent in pleasure
And laughing at the smiles I meet rocking in your arms so sweet.
As time will slowly pass along the labour of my love grows strong,
I look upon you lovingly because you mean so much to me,
Linger longer with me lay for sweetest joy is mine today
Your face my angel I adore the very sight I seek the more,
How I think to love you so are thoughts that only angels know.
To be with you is heaven's bliss upon your lips a gentle kiss
No woman had such tender arms or looked at me with girlish charms.
Holding you is so sublime a happier fate could not be mine
That love which stirred our hearts in youth,
will always grow in peaceful truth.
While you're not with me it seems I can still hold you in my dreams,
When from you I am away even for one single day,
A roaring tempest fills me vain only you can ease the pain.
I know you will not let me perish a stronger love could not cherish,
I'd love so much the Summer days when holding you in window bays.
The nights we wished for soon to kiss again in light of moon.
All grace and beauty like a rose you are my love from head to toes.
No other way could it ever be but such sweet thoughts always with me,
One tiny teardrop from your eye makes me feel I want to die,
No matter what mistakes we make oh promise me my wedding cake.

V M Rockliff

Our Tree

Emotional words form endlessly on the paper,
Telling an unfamiliar story,
Of heartbreaks unknown and of autumn leaves,
That fall for an eternity to the whispering wind.

The dark, solitary leaves imitate my forgotten soul,
And the wind that carelessly comforts, carries me home,
Alone,
The harsh unnatural light would seem cold and impersonal,
Compared to the candle we used to share,
And so the moon shyly creeps through my window.

The turn of seasons, heals aching emotions,
And the very same branch that shed its leaves,
Returns, with tiny, new parts of me, uncurling before my eyes,
The complete branch joins the tree to form a whole picture.

When the summer comes around,
And we grow old,
We shade ourselves beneath the tree,
Hanging our tired feet in cool waters,
We see not the tree,
But a reflection of our love.

Hannah Sigley

Mum

To me the word mum means love.
A word much stronger than God above
A mum is someone who is always there
Willing to love, give and share.

To me the word mum means friend
A broken heart something mum would mend
She will be there for you through thick and thin
A mum is something you simply cannot win.

To me my mum is the best
Much better than all the rest
My mum has not ever said an unkind word
At least not one that I have heard.

Julie Walker (14)

Small Verse

'I'm not afraid,'
'Brave words,' you said,
'I'm willing to join the multi dead.'

'My fears are laid,'
'for now,' you said.
'I'm tired of living from a bed.'

'My will is made,'
'Who cares?' you said.
'I'll not be here when it is read.'

But life held on. Love held me fast
Until such morbid thoughts were past.

Joyce Harrington

Betrayal

It came upon me suddenly
Tugging like a beggar at my sleeve.
Beneath the seemingly still, calm waters of our lives -
This malignant serpent of doubt lay waiting
- Coiled like a spring in the deep, dark recess of my complacency

I stumbled blindly on
In blissful ignorance of your betrayal.
Knowledge, when it came, was bittersweet
Bringing tearful apologies, second chances
And yet . . .
And yet . . .
In the stark, hesitant newness of a rekindled flame
The fangs remain embedded
Discreetly eroding our tomorrows with acidic venom.

Yvonne Roberts

Fair Game

My love is only cupboard love
yet . . .
when you come home, tired from walking,
(who knows where?)
I run to greet you, nudge you, sniff you,
making noises of delight
at your slab-icy fish, your bald meat,
while you smile and talk and stroke
and share your game with me.
But why . . .
when I come home, tense from stalking,
triumphant with my pond-fresh carp,
or feral trophy
do you become displeased, stop smiling
and simply throw the thing away?

Anita Holmes

Nocturne

What lips my lips have kissed and
where and why, I have forgotten, and
what arms have lain under my head.
But the rain is full of ghosts tonight
that tap and sigh upon the glass and
listen for replies.
I cannot say what loves have come and gone -
I only know that Summer sang for me a little
while but sings for me no more.

Barbara Stiles

My Child

You came to me from the unknown
'Twas Spring that season fair
A spark divine and mine the task
To train and tend with care

This spirit in His image made
Expansion of His love
We may accept or we reject
This gift from Heaven above

I knew 'twould not be always Spring
Snow ever follows sun
And clouds tho' then invisible
Some time would surely come

And so to shield you from the winds
Of envy, hate and strife
I've wrapped round you a cloak of love
Which shall outlast this life

And should another cross your path
Whose heart is filled with care
This cloak shall wipe away all tears
So with Him gladly share.

Daisy Hale

Yesterday

I'd love to get back yesterday,
Recall the love I sent away,
I'd love to hear his voice again,
The very first, a prior claim,
He had a voice, I loved to hear,
A special smile I held so dear,
In youth we did expect so much,
Ambition, parting, out of touch,
I'd love to get back yesterday,
To feel his loving gentle ways,
How well he knew me, understood,
My fickle ways, my changing mood,
We did meet up, in later years,
Talking, laughing, voicing fears,
Knowing time would claim its due,
And me not there to comfort you,
Just being there, to hold your hand,
No need for words, I'd understand
I'd love to get back yesterday,
I'm wiser now, I'd beg you stay.

E F Calderwood

Our End

I do not love him. There is nothing there.
Yet inside me is a sea of despair,
I didn't ever mean to *ruin* his life.
But I can't stay his wife.

His fantasy world, his complete life dream
Revolved round a house and me it would seem.
Oh, forget my life, it wasn't mine to live
Just a bauble to give.

Imagine, if we'd still been together
Redundancy a hard storm to weather . . .
A move back *home*, feel my impotent rage
Hear the close of my cage.

I feel like a hangman - I've cut him dead
I've thrown back the lot - all the vows we said.
He made me so sad - I had to get free
Have a chance to be me.

Debbie Hilton

A Letter to my Love

An empty place where I was fed
A rounded pillow where once my head
Did lie and sleep and dream upon
But now no more for I am gone.

No pain but peace now fills my shell
If I could speak to you I'd tell
To wipe those tears that stain your eyes
And clear away my shirts and ties.

For life for you must still proceed
Along the road for those who need
Your kindness, warmth, the urge to help
Those empty hearts like one's bare shelf.

For time will come when pain has flown
And you will feel not all alone
And laughter once again will sound
From the one I love left on the ground.

Douglas Arthur

I Called it Love

I called it love,
but lied,
for it was desperation -
that knowledge
that a night would come,
so dark,
that it would drown the stars;
a fear of falling blinded
into emptiness.
And, when I clung to you,
I was clinging
with the terror of a child
afraid of being left
to sleep alone.

I called it love,
but lied.

Vivien Payne

Smile of Love

Why do you smile at me my love
We have covered so many miles in life's journey through the years
So many treasured memories we have shared and still you smile
I love you oh! so very much
I never can express enough, of all my thoughts surrounding you
Hopes and dreams that never did come true
And still you smile
So take my hand 'til life is ore
Together we will smile at all that is in store

Lena Doherty

You

(Dedicated to Stan my inspiration)

You came into my stormy life
And calm into it brought
You are deep within my heart
And occupy each thought

You came just when I needed you
And by my side you stood
You gave me tender love and care
More than you really should

You gave me your true friendship
And into more it grew
You wiped away my teardrops
When I was feeling blue

You showed me how to love
Again when all inside was dead
You tenderly encouraged me
With loving things you said

You made me trust you gave me
Strength where once I was so weak
You patiently helped me to confide
And to open up and speak

You gave me so much of yourself
In your strong and silent way
You gave me hope within my self
To face each coming day

You left but you're still with
Me it sounds hard to explain
You are in my thoughts you're in my
Heart and that's where you'll remain

You made me feel so good inside
It's silly but it's true
You should be proud of what you
Did just by being *'you'*

C A Hewitson

Sad Goodbye

We wouldn't kiss in public,
in a normal situation.
But wartime was a crisis time,
so we kissed at the station.

Though we were private people,
we kissed and clung together.
Knowing that this parting,
might be forever.

We spent our leave together,
every precious second.
Wanting it to never end,
but our duty beckoned.

So we parted at the station,
promising to write.
And that we'd be true,
then returned to the fight.

Elsie Margaret Watt

Untitled

Oh, Nan what can I do to take this hurt away,
To stop the tears, that fill my heart with dismay,
I thought you'd live a hundred years,
Never realising everlasting life was drawing near.
You know we always loved you, we did not have to say,
And I know you loved us in your very special way,
So we pray you will be happy and find eternal peace at last,
But don't forget there will always,
Be a place for you in our hearts.

Denise Tong

You, me and Everything

Have you ever loved your Daddy?
but your soul just won't cool down;
at least that's how it seems,
when an unknown love is back in town,
and the touch you always long for,
just doesn't seem to be around.

So gently ask Sweet Mary;
to away the pain;
after all, She is a Mother,
so it can't remain the same.
Thank God, I still love you,
because at least that way I know,
although I'm still a little lost,
She'll show me where to go.

Live for Christ's sake, always;
then go out to all and give;
when you think you've done it all;
live for Christ's sake - live!

I'm high as high can be, in the
town where I write your name,
and it's right next to yours,
but you only see it in the rain.

Somewhere there's a broken heart,
with a slightly broken mind,
and still I ask: 'Who can it be?'
then I see it's mine.

Don't worry - there's a turning point,
and it will come to you;
a light that still shines bright,
and everything that's true.
If you don't know how to pray;
just turn around and kiss the ground;
let Him softly say to you;
'I love you friend, I really do.'

Jan Krupa

First Romance

It's happened at last, can it be true
She is so pretty, what can I do,
She could so easily break his heart
So should I speak. How would I start.
I could explain, he's very young
Hardly learned to use his tongue.
Not ready yet to get involved
But talking won't get my problem solved.
I really can't bear it,
It's breaking my heart.
I can't understand how it all came to start
I must dry my tears if I'm going to win
I'll sit right down and open a tin.
I'll show that miss, and that is that
For Tom is mine. My tabby-cat.

P Howard

Parting - a Wallow

It was last week that we parted.
Last week we said goodbye
And you are gone, gone from my life
And I'm left wondering why.

It seems like only yesterday,
When you left me in the rain,
And now I feel the sorrow
The anguish and the pain.

What did I love about you
Apart from your sweet smile?
Each night I pray we'll meet again
In just a little while.

It is your Kiss
I miss each night
It is your tender care
It is so hard to realise
That now you are not there.

Each night in the gloom
Of my empty room
I shan't stop shedding tears.
My sorrow I know will never cease
Through the advancing years.

Come back my dear
Come back to me.
Don't leave me here alone,
I'll wait for you forever,
Oh please, oh please
Come home.

Myra Green

How Much do I Care

Ask me, my Dearest, how much do I care.
  But it's not so easy to say.
Much more than the snow flakes that drift from the sky,
  on a cold and wintry day.
My love is much larger than all of the seas,
  and deeper than the deepest of them.
And take all the diamonds and emeralds and pearls,
  it's still greater than the most precious gem.

But no way can we measure the depth of a love,
  or a strength of a bond that exists.
For devotion and love are like gossamer wings.
  Touch them roughly, they'll melt in the mist.
But rare though it is, there can come perfect love,
  but it comes to only a few.
Who are touched by the magic of God's precious gift,
  which I share in my great love for you.

So that is the answer I give to you now,
  my love is greater than life.
But it's not just my love, but our love that counts,
  and the fact we are husband and wife.
Who share a perfection that bonds us as one,
  for each other we always are there.
For you are my life and I am your life,
  so that is how much we both care.

M Bathgate

An Apology

No matter how I try
No matter what I do
I always seem to get it wrong
And end up hurting you
Forgive me one more time
I know I've caused you pain
But it was not intentional
Just lack of thought again
Whatever else I say
Whatever else I do
What matters most above all else
Is just that I love you

Angie Mathieson

First Born

I never understood why you hated me,
You seemed to delight in making me cry,
You made sure I knew you had the power
To decide whether I'd live or die.

You crushed all the innocence out of me,
You hit me with every word that you spoke
Yet I loved you as every child loves their parent
And clung to the faint light of hope.

I foolishly thought I could make you love me,
For years I tried my hardest to win
Your affection, tolerance, understanding,
Your praise for something, anything.

Time passed, the situation worsened,
As I grew, so did your disdain,
It became harder to hide my emotions
- That only provoked you again.

And now I've finally realised
I'm fighting a battle that cannot be won.
I can never be the perfect daughter
If all you want is a son.

Stephanie Lewis

To Die in Love

A pounding heart beats within my chest,
When I look at you it feels no rest,
Your hair and face, the way you walk,
You keep me alive and then you talk.
A mouth so perfect - on such a face
It rests and opens with a swan's grace.
This distant world in which I live,
Feeds my passion which I want to give.
My eyes are closed and you're all I see,
Your gentle hand holds my heart's key.
This blinding love will stay inside
Alas in you I cannot confide.
In this tunnel there is a glimpse of light
It is the end of a cold lonely night,
And so I bid you a fond farewell
As I hear them ring that final bell,
The dawn is breaking along with my heart
As I whisper 'I Love You,' they tear us apart.

Alexandra Richardson

My Prayer

Lord let her heart incline to mine
and make her true, for love
and not for pity's sake
and if her thoughts should ever start to roam
as girls thoughts will
Let her remember home.
Not as four walls where duty bids her stay
But as a haven at the close of day.
Let not the circle of her wedding ring
A sense of shackles or of bondage bring.
As years roll on and we are growing old
And life is like a tale that has been told
May I in my little daughters see
Some likeness of the girl she used to be
And in the features of each precious face
Find what I loved in her of charm and grace
And may we, when this life itself shall cease
Embrace thee, Lord, together in eternal
peace.

John Michael McIntyre

To my Love

Loved face ethereal faint is the dusk of your hair
And gently half fearing to touch thee, explore with my lips
That curve where the shadow lies deep and the throat lies bare
While the passion that pulses my soul puts the world in eclipse.

When we walk those long miles in the spell of the night
And I bend down to kiss the dew from your cheek
The laughter that gleams in those emerald eyes
Is the pledge that I need for the love that I seek.

Some flowers that bloom in their season are plucked
But our love is so sure that no one can take.
It transcends the four seasons and spans the wide Earth
A happiness mirrored in each Moon ravished lake.

Alan Gray

My Lover

A man has just passed through my life,
I'm feeling lonely, upset, crushed and broken,
For a while he talked and I was special and pretty,
He smiled and I was worthy to be touched,
He sought my body and explored it with passion,
He was the centre of my life, with me every waking moment,
Now he is gone and I am not special any more,
I didn't love him and wanted him to leave,
But now I miss the happy past times,
We sit together, but far apart longing to be touched.

Pamela Reed

Woman

Woman she listens, your needs she will tend.
Please give in return; woman is friend.
Woman she loves you, just you, not another.
Cherish her love; woman is lover.

Woman she cares for, and helps you through life.
Care for her too; woman is wife.
Woman she gives, a life to another.
Your children they live. Woman is mother.

Stephen J Fellows

My Wishes and Maybe Yours

I wish I could be with you
Each minute of the day
I wish you would not leave me
When I want you to stay

I wish that you could love me
When we both feel it is right
I wish that we could make love
Each and every night

I wish that we could laugh and run
Over the hills in leaps and bounds
I wish that we could go home
When the milkman's making his rounds

I wish I'd met you years ago
And not just yesterday
I wish that when I pass away
You could wish for me to stay

I wish our wishes could come true
You could wish for me and I could wish for you.

Benjamin Davidson

Untitled

To be far away
Was hard from the start
And the pain that I feel
Almost breaking my heart
So I send you a poem
On the wings of a dove
So while I am away
You can read of my love
This love that I send
A love that is true
To those that I miss most.
This love is for you.

John Nicholls

Little Lost Love

The empty cot stands
In the silent room.
Stained and knotted floor boards
Creak with the first step.
A breeze rustles the muslin curtain
And delicately wafts a single white feather
To the floor.
All is still now
Save my beating heart.
Sweet memory meanders
Back to childhood . . .
To the tousle-haired toddler
Who puffs a dandelion clock
And waits . . .
While fragile, flimsy fluff
Floats far away
Like lovers lost
In fond farewell.

Anita Crisp

Love and Need

I know I'm *loved*, a
beautiful word

I am not *needed*, an
ugly word.

My children *love* me
but do not *need* me

My friends *love* me
but do not *need* me

I *love* them all -
but I am not needed.

What do I want?
I want to be *needed!*

Ann Collins

Last Words

Evensong bells from St Mary's had sounded,
Across the wet fields, through the mist and the gloom.
From Harrow's hill, with dripping trees all surrounded,
Down to the station and the cold waiting room.
Where I waited with Penny for her train to Wendover,
Our secret affair like the summer was over.

In the silence and sadness we breathed not a word,
Of the feelings we had of the love that we shared.
Those impossible dreams, so blind and absurd,
Lay broken in pieces as our two hearts despaired.
On that October evening in the damp autumn chills,
Penny was leaving for The Chiltern Hills.

We sat holding hands till the Aylesbury train,
Took her into the darkness down the glistening lines.
Back to her husband, and her sad life again,
Back to the cottage where the sun never shines.
Two words and she'd have stayed, two words never said,
I was left alone on the platform, with the words in my head.

Ron Lamerton

Lovely Light

My love, don't let this lovely light die
sweet light I have never known before.
This pure precious light cannot be a lie
radiance so exquisite, come, show me more.

No love, don't let this lovely light fade,
come, help me feed its glow with love.
Don't let your horror of life's lonely jade
murder this light, sent to us from above.

Let the beautiful light shine from your eyes
as it shines from my eyes for you.
This matchless light could never be lies
come, let's give life to its glory anew.

Oh Phil, don't turn from love and light,
let your heart and spirit see it is good.
Don't hide in the darkness afraid to fight
come, let it flow in a glorious flood.

No love, don't leave me in cold dark night
don't make this light faded and tarnished.
Together we'll fill the cosmos with light,
darkness and pain would ever be vanquished.

Joan Ames

War of our Hearts

The quietest moment
I have ever experienced
Was between the shots
As silently we lay
Thinking the same thoughts

Together we felt
An uneasy silence
When we were spent
We just lay
Silently

Somewhere between
Loneliness and companionship
You my comrade in arms
By my side
On the damp battlefield

With our eyes avoiding contact
Dreading that someone should speak
Fearful of the surrounding quiet
A fence of barbed wire between us
A special bond still linked us

And in the years to come
If I should see you
The world would turn silent
And we would not speak
Survivors both

Michael A Stewart

Come Back

With the promise of another
With the blow of the kiss
With the arms of which I hold you
It's those feelings that I miss

I long for you to hold me
To take me through the night
To catch me on collision
To become one, a feeling of right

Your hands that caress me
Up and down my spine
Taking in my passions
Making us entwine

So come to me, return
Take me through your days
I long for your personal touch
To undress me in your ways

Take away this hardened skin
And come to me in haze
Darling forever love me
In these short and darkened days

Daniel Golding

Untitled

'Tis a while since I disdained from thee
my privy friend
But, then again we both do know
that we'll be together at the end.
Answer me this question
so that my feelings I can send.
And halt this emotion that hath driven me
since the first time when
we two were coincided and joined together.
Until the wrath of God would see us forever,
Until the day shall come when we should finally part,
That day shall come when though shalt empty
all of my heart.

Paul Brook

Mockery

The untouchable love
The love you dare not touch
Or dare not love
Is the sweetest and sincerest

Fate throws lovers together
And sits up there, laughing
Making a mockery of our hearts
And pulling us apart.

Elizabeth H Walter

The Unknown Child

To my unknown child,
Who left so soon,
Without a single goodbye.
I wish I could tell you,
I loved you so . . .
Even though you were unborn.

Were you a girl?
Were you a boy?
This is something I'll never know
But how I still miss you, even today
You leave me wandering, all the time

You were a person, someone special
Whom I never had the chance to know
Yet, from the very beginning I loved you
And now you'll never know, how much
I miss you, or how much I love you still.

Pravina Patel

This Rainbow of Mine

My love, my only and my light
Wears red for courage, his will, his energy;
Orange, the colour of a flame in the dark of night;
Yellow, for his wisdom, his strength intellectually;
Green for balance, peace and harmonic insight;
Blue, calm waters, his trust and faith in me;
Indigo, his loyalty, power and noble might;
Violet, for he gives and loves unselfishly.

My love has virtues from all the rays,
And as Richard of York gave battle in vain,
My love brightens my life in the darkest of days,
Without war or strife, his colours remain
Aglow in his aura, and in his ways.
I prey to God that I still may gain
His love and his love of life for always,
Eternally beyond death, insanity or pain.

Gillian C Stone

I am Your Music

Play me, I am your music, your song,
You are the one for whom I long
Turn my pages, use my score
You are the one that I adore.
Like a piano with so many keys,
You are the one, I so want to please.
So take me in your arms,
Give to me of your charms,
I am your orchestra, your symphony
So my love, Play me, Play me.

P Smith

Affair in Hell

She was in love;
But too afraid to tell.
The guilt clung like glue
As the shame of it
Made her shiver right through;
She was afraid,
Scared of this affair in hell,
She could have been happy;
But dared not let go.
No one knew her pain
Or the sordid secrets
Of her life's sorry game;
She was repelled,
Ashamed of her show.
And the girl of her dreams
Came gently to mind,
And she smiled, and she cried,
And made herself blind;
She was hidden,
Hiding from the lies.
The guilt clung like glue
And the loneliness
Made her shiver right through;
She was afraid,
That a man might see through her cries.

Anna Paul

Love

What is this *Love* that you talk about?
Is it really an emotional force from within?
Or is it really a spiritual lout?
A lout that poses our minds and souls and dominates every
decision in our pattern of thinking - It can change your entire life!

Maybe we are all fooled by this false sense of security, like
pulling the wool over your eyes.
Conquer love and you have conquered your life, your world.

What foolish words we portray onto ourselves;
Since we have all seen the state of destitution too, that this force will
create

A person who has experienced too much Love

A Prajapat

A Memory of you

I used to be scared and fear,
The day I would have to leave,
This special and beautiful world around me,
All the loved ones I would no longer see.

But one day I shall never forget,
You said something that touched my heart,
When I realised your life was slipping away,
And had to accept that we will soon part.

You told me that if such a world,
Could be made where we met for the first time in the past,
There must be a land for us to rest,
And come together forever at last.

Claire Crossley (13)

Nan

Only one before you,
Had my love in such a way,
One before you,
Could brighten up my day,
You took the place of your lost child,
You shared with me your love,
And now you are reunited;
With your daughter,
In Heaven above.
I know you're, looking down on me,
I know you're having fun.
Dancing down the milky way
With Grandad and Mom.

M S Cornbill

Young Nell Gwynne

Oh rollicking frolicking winsome young Nell
With voice so alluring and clear as a bell.
Enchanting as songbird above on the wing,
How could she not capture the heart of a King.

Oh sweet pretty, gay witty, saucy young Nell
Her luscious bright oranges selling so well,
Her beauty surpassing the freshness of Spring,
'Twas no wonder she'd captured the heart of a King.

Oh spry little, fly little, sly little Nell,
The pride of Old Drury wherein she did dwell.
She cared not a whit that she lacked a gold ring.
What more could she need than the heart of a King!

Celia White

Remember

Remember the way he whistled as he turned his key in the door.
Remember the way he wore slippers in the garden -
And muddy shoes indoors.
Remember how often he said 'I love you' with
words and looks and ways.
Remember how he'd peel oranges for me and
butter my toast on Sundays.
Remember the way he seldom laughed
aloud - or shouted or raved.
Remember his strength, his quiet calm -
The rows we had over cutting the lawn.
How we talked all night when our sons were born.
The stubble when he wouldn't shave.
Remember how it felt to know that someone always cared.
I remember.

Olive Portsmouth

Untitled

Rejection - that's my only friend
We lay together, and remember how we met.
You introduced us - about the time you left,
And now we're eternal companions.
Rejection has agreed to leave if you
Return to me, but that can never be
And so - inexplicably bound
We live on.

Julie Palmer

Dug From the Night

The room was cold like ice through my mind
The wind outside blew with the rain,
Until she entered and sat by my side
The warmth of her eyes erased all my pain.
Serenely, her voice came like the tide,
Eyes with such passion were now sweetly tame,
Through the violent gales she was my guide
Her beauty would put the sunset to shame.

The time will pass,
These screaming winds won't drag you away,
Our time at last
Will come as soon as it was washed away,
And I don't care for society's lies,
The city will take you
Like bright blue eyes
Way up to the skies, our time is true.

Why I should be so silent and coy
When seeing this child of fatherhood joy.

My thoughts reflected in her face,
Her aspect lifted me in the night,
A complexion, soft, as pure as lace
Nothing was wrong and everything right,
'Til she had to leave, my thoughts left to chase
The wonderful girl who made darkness bright.

Robert Wilson

The Crush

If I could voice his virtues
'Twould be a litany of love
Mom scoffs 'infatuation'
Dad grunts 'just puppy love'
But they don't know the magic
Of hearing music in the maths
And of sums becoming symphonies
I know they think I'm daft
'A silly crush' laughs my big sister
'You're only ten plus four
He must be nearer forty
You'll get over it for sure'
Of arithmetic he's the preacher
I am his adoring pupil
And he is my unaware teacher

Violet Hoare

My Dream

As I lay down my head at night
I wonder what is wrong or right
I think about a lady dear
and wish that she was lying near.

A tear doth trickle down my cheek
with lump in throat it's hard to speak
How much I miss her know I not
A memory that's hard to blot.

Why do we have to be apart
Doth ask this ache within my heart
Does she know I need her so
or is it just to make me go.

Come be with me my love I say
this moment forth and every day
For I will never break your heart
or trouble you for us to part.

So don't you ever despair my love
My dreams of you come from above
I see your beauty it's hard to tell
It's like a magic cast, a spell.

But then, a sudden turn, a jolt
I waken like a thunderbolt
A look, a glance, and you're not there
the room is cold, empty and bare.

This dream will never go away
That you'll be there with me one day
So with these words I say to you
Come back my love and make them true.

Brian S Berger

Now I Know

Standing at the riverside
Under the blue black shadow of a yew tree
I look into the river for answers
A fractured image stares back at me

I wanted you so much
My child, as yet unborn
Today I must decide

Am I wrong to make you live?
Some say I am
With a life filled with turmoil

Your father has left me all alone
Yet strangely I don't feel forlorn

Must I inflict all this on you?
And the poverty to which you will be heir

Pondering this and more
I look hard at the yew tree
Its trunk blackened by a lightning strike
Forever in my mind the lightning tree

Yet still it grows
Reminding me of God
And the part he played in this
Of the plan for you and me

Kay Dumont

A Soldier Who'll Never Arrive

Smiling meekly she waits,
Waiting for a soldier who'll never arrive.
Her knuckles white with the pain of crossed fingers.

She glances around, but sees no crowds.
The crowds waiting, the same as she.
All she sees is the empty ocean;
And the rain slow to drizzle.

The announcement comes long overdue,
The words crisp, yet sad.
The sounds come out as foreign words.
The cries rise, they shall not return.

Age old is the action of mothers and wives,
Age old their fears and cries.

Samantha Duff

Untitled

The rapture of my passion
is ever lost in your eyes,
my desire of your tenderness grows nearer,
but the absence of your heart on mine is forever longing.

J D Laverty

Dying Love

The words I write are those which are given,
to pine a gentle phrase,
The sweet lips I kissed,
I remember well . . .
Your perfume . . . the fragrance,
of a whispering meadow,
We would walk hand-in-hand, without a care
lying in the corn,
with little money, living on each other's love.

I may be a soldier, but I
cried myself to sleep,
without a tear,
War is more than this,
we fight to honour our country,
burying friends along the way.
Serg says, 'Actions speak louder than words,'
well the words are dying, they'll soon be rid.

So I lie on a hospital bed
thinking of you in your red dress.
With your blond hair flowing, with your melting smile.
So here I lie, won't last 'til dawn,
my baby son that I leave,
please God, don't let him forget me.
You'll always be in my thoughts,
I'll lisp thy name though dying,
The Woman I have always loved.
Your Darling, Love.

D L Phillips

Love's Wonder

Enraptured with pure wonder
I gaze upon the world
with endless fascination.
Time has stood still -
nay - the years have rolled back,
for now mine is the
innocence of childhood
whose eyes alone can see
and appreciate the beauty
which old eyes never could.
To make friends of rain,
storm and wind.
Walking wetly through
showers of sheer pleasure -
an eccentricity overshadowed
only by the joy of being
playfully pushed and brushed
by the refreshing tempest.
What gains the sophistication
of maturing years
over nature's simple childjoys?

Leslie Thomas

Beyond Tears

Loneliness
settles like a mist
sometimes rising
sometimes falling
with the unpredictableness
of the wind.
How often do I roam this
empty house
vainly awaiting your call.
As realisation dawns
Despair takes over
Like a light sky
darkening to blackest night.
Life's walk is short
and bitter.
The golden bowl
held out before you
so full of brightness and promise
is shown to be
empty and vain.
The highest joys of love
only mask the
deepest pains of adversity.
To be loved
but never quite enough
to be worth
giving all.

Christine Kerslake

Tumbled Words

I wish that I could speak the words
Which tumble in my brain.
Words of love and how I long
To touch your hair again.

Tell how my heart will miss a beat
When you smile and take my hand
Or how bright the day when I see you
So you will understand.

I want to speak about our love
And all the joy it brings.
Would I could untumble words
To tell you all these things.

Patricia Catling

New Year Dance 1977

Held in a net of time
My multicoloured, fragile dreams
Float high above the circling dancers,
Moving by custom, or chance, or love
To the music of this plastic age.

A spotlight moves to catch your beauty
Glowing above the debris of a littered table
And, for an instant, I see such heartbreak in your glance
And somehow know your past is very near.

Looking, but not looking,
Intuition tells of what I could not, should not know.
Each eggshell dream crushed
By what is not said, not heard, not seen.

Midnight.
And in a wave of singing, hugging, kisses and false promises
My dreams fall into this bitter sea.
Seized by one you love
And, like your heart,
Broken thoughtlessly.

Ray Bedford

Dancing Hearts Dame Margot Fonteyn and Rudolf Nureyev

Snowy plains of Russia brought him, to melt
our western hearts.
The ember passion'd talent flared his dance with
youthful art.
Theatre wings relinquished *Margot,* she took
my breath away.
Her delicate warm refinement, thistledown steps
of a summer's day.
The romance of fire and sunlight, scattering dance
and beauty sublime.
Two spirits, two worlds encompassed, dancing hearts
in eternal time.

Doreen Morris

Night and Day

Today the dark clouds flew away,

'I love you so,' I heard him say,

'And by your side I want to stay,'

And night turned into day,
And wrong to right,
And black to white,
And blind to sight,
And dark to light,
I reached the height
Of pure delight -
I'd won the fight.

Today the dark clouds flew away,

'I love you best,' I heard him say,

'The price is not too high to pay,'

And night turned into day.

M J Carter

A Foreign Tale

The multitude of spires reached into the skies,
Ancient buildings and bridges stood in splendour;
Symbols of a nobler bygone age.
The ghosts of the city watched the plot unfold,
A story they had seen many times before.

I remember the love blaze in her eyes.
We dined by candlelight to violins;
We walked arm in arm in the glow of the street lamps,
Upon the damp echoic cobblestones.

We gazed down at the city
From the castle high above.
Neither dwelling among men, nor the Gods:
We had found a kingdom of our own.

A thousand times we promised love 'til death;
Parting in sorrow, sealed with pledges of faith.

Now the sirens call me upon the rocks,
To smash our love.
With red lips and painted faces,
Flowing hair and exotic perfumes,
Admiring glances and silken smiles.
Guilty in thought, but innocent in deed,
I wonder . . .
          Am I worthy of the love in her eyes?
The ancient ghosts whisper an inaudible reply.

Anon

Untitled

Living by the sea you sailed into my heart.
My harbour since has drained, yet
You remain so anchored there,
Stranded above the tide of reason
On a rocky, shingle beach of love.
Here the moon pulls, not the seas,
Nor the winds entice the waves,
A calm of pure tranquillity abounds
Unrequited love swaddled in silent sound
Unstirred even by desire's breeze.

'Tis distance that becalms us thus,
Uncertain territories of the other's mind means
Supposition alone survives a watery clime.
In this solitude of companionship
Drifting ever onwards with the current
To the ocean pond of perpetual peace.

Prudence Heritage

I'm Covered Now

Walking in grey streets yesterday,
I thought I saw you.
But I could hardly see you,
Through the wall of friends I'm still building.
Strange to think,
This sturdy wall,
Was once so thin,
It would evaporate before my eyes,
If you were near.
But that was long ago,
Before others declared,
Their hearts:
When our two souls touched,
And danced in naked firelight,
Became Gods:
Isis-Osiris: Gold-skinned girl-boys,
We loved with pagan ecstasy,
And warred with pagan jealousy,
Were made mortal.
Yet, I still recall,
The taste of sweet, destructive limbs,
We wrote our own mythology.
But you are indistinct,
A vision blurred beyond my strange defence,
Beyond my wall of friends,
I cannot reach you.
I'm covered now.

Nicola Harlow

Love

How should I feel, now you have gone?
I loved you for so very long.
Where does love go, when two lives divide?
I know that my love for you survived.
The love that we had cannot be destroyed
But without you to hold me, there is such a void.

Our love grew much stronger, day after day,
But now we're apart, it can't just fade away.
Your love's all around me - I bask in its warmth,
It's in the brightness of colours and in music, it haunts.

I'm aware of your presence, I feel your soft breath.
Can it be true that we do survive death?
Love's universal, the source of all life
And even in death, you're the love of my life.

Alan Seymour

Of Memories Past

The billowing clouds form overhead,
So I gather myself and head for the shed,
And sit midst old newspapers round about spread,
Then drift off and let fantasy fill my head.

The hypnotic thud of rain on the roof,
Sends me back in time to a part of my youth,
Of when I was thirty, and so much in love,
With a woman who surely had come from above.

I can see us now sitting, gazing out o'er the view,
The sun for us shone and the sky was pure blue,
I see us sat talking on steps near a pool,
And remember then thinking that love has no rules.

My thoughts then drift to another scene,
And some other place that we had been,
I see the blankets there outspread,
With two indentations where we had led.

The mood was perfect, and again the sun shone,
The place was deserted, we were now on our own,
With wine uncorked, and the sun up above,
We sipped, we laughed and we made love.

But in my dreams a soft voice spake,
I start to stir and slowly wake,
And then fix my eyes upon tea and cake,
I feel a warmth inside.

I stand and turn, my love's now here,
With her I've come to know no fear,
My life I'll live, right to the last,
And fill my dreams with memories past.

Rob Baston

The Meaning of Love

Who knows the meaning of love?
A four lettered word.
It causes pain and tears.
In the hearts of many, it brings fear.

Love is a word of trust,
of beauty, wise and good.
Of all those I have loved,
no-one competes with your love.

Love is a four lettered word,
I don't care which you choose.
For if I ever win in love,
one day you're bound to lose.

Neil Watkins

Out of Nowhere

I cannot believe this love I've found
Was really meant to be.
He came from out of 'nowhere',
Reached out his hand to me.
My heart skipped a beat and then
His lips I felt on mine.
Be my love forever, let it last the test of time
Were his very words, 'Marry me,' he said.
In a tiny country church he and I were wed.
It didn't last for very long
Back to 'nowhere' he went
But for a fleeting moment
I was magically content.

B Lake

Images of Love

If I could climb the stair of gold,
  What glories would I there behold;
A sight of remembered face,
  Would speed my soul, the stairs to race,
And time, I hope, would freeze awhile,
  That lovely enigmatic smile:
But that dear face, now disappears,
  I shout - and think that no-one hears.

Les Mortlock

Miscarriage

So lost and lonely
So alone and dark
Too little to know
Or have known.

Never knew the light
Or joy of play
Or warmth of holding,

Never learnt hot or cold
Black or white
Boy or girl,

Never learnt religion,
Its truths, its wars,
Its kindness.

Maybe next time.

Janet Hughes

A Perfect Duplicity

I no longer possess a name:
she has stolen it away from me,
and owns my very soul.

All that is human, all that is remotely
of this earth, her love has neutralised;
leaving only that which really matters.

My soul, free from its petty constraints,
the concerns of possessing a name,
rising to rejoice in the theft:

And I am glad;
a willing culprit in this perfect duplicity;
glad to be coveted and cherished by love.

Paul Megycks

Flowers I Shall Send

Flowers I shall send without a name
That none can tell wherefrom they came
And when you gaze upon their hue
Remember me and the love I send to you.

Their petals will be soft to your touch
And tell that I miss you so much
And they will be gently speckled with dew
To remind of the tears I cry for you.

In their midst will linger a rose
Of the deepest red that nature knows
And it will come straight from my heart
For all the time that we are apart.

And as the petals fall to the floor
I shall love you all the more
For what we have will eternally be
Though you will never belong just to me.

Barbara A Percy

When you Said it was Over

When you said it was over
I pretended not to hear,
Humming quietly to myself
Your words were unclear.

Grabbing me by the arm
You said you were leaving
I continued ignoring you,
My mind was disbelieving.

When your bags were packed
And standing by the door,
I went into the kitchen,
Began to wash the floor.

Still humming I looked away
When you walked up to me,
Pleading for a hearing
Before you turned to flee.

When the front door slammed
My humming became intense,
When I shut out your words
It was for my own defence.

On the bathroom mirror
I found the note you left,
My humming stopped abruptly
My reflection openly wept.

Keely Nethercott

Inconsistency

There was a time - so long ago -
When i could call you mine.
That time your face on me would grow
Like a melody on rhyme.

There was a time - the clock of life
Ticks on - when you were everything,
All I struggled for and the strife
Was summoned just to hear you sing.

Still that time - that vain inglorious space
Of life - was never meant to be,
The rapture wrapped up in your face
Was inconsistency.

Uilleam Brus Moireasdan - Mac-'ille-mhoire.

W B Morison

End the Fight

Hello, my love on this dark night,
hold my hand and make it light!

You were my brightness, you were my light.
Now you're my shadow in the night.
There isn't reason on which I can call,
for I have known you, if at all.

Goodbye my lover, farewell my light.
Forgive me, kiss me . . .
and end the fight.

R J Rapkins

Comparisons

Today I brought you a rose
As you lay fast asleep
I placed it on your pillow
To show my love, so deep.
And then I knew comparisons
Could never yet be true,
Because the rose looked wilted
As it lay close to you.

Its colour, form and faint perfume
Looked perfect on the bush,
But yet it could not even match
Your sweet and gentle blush.
I thought the dew lay twinkling
On its petals 'neath the sky,
And that still failed to equal
The sparkle in your eye.

No flower in the garden
Or in all the world, so far
Can give me as much pleasure
As to just be where you are
The marvels of the universe
Are all set out to view
Yet I can think of only one.
And she my love, is you.

John Arnold Hilton

My Home Port

I've always been in love
With my home port
Through the winter months
The sea air keeps the snow away
In the summer week
The salt air keeps the pollen down
I've always had room in my heart
For my home port
Wherever in the world
I find myself
My roots will always be here
Amongst the seaweed and the sand.

I've always been in love
With my home port
On the shifting sand
I think that 'Time and Tide' have left
For the final time
New ideas clash with old ways
I've always had room in my heart
For my home port
Wherever in the world
I find myself
My roots will always be here
Amongst the seaweed and the sand.

David Young

Kiss Him so Gently

Oh kiss him so gently for me
For the world says I haven't the right
It says that our love should never have been
That's why I've stepped down from the fight

I have to deny that I love him,
I have to pretend that I don't,
I've tried my best to hurt him
So to take of his love I won't.

I sit back and watch them all smiling
I'll never tell them I'm dead,
I'll play their charade the way they say
They won't see the tears that I shed.

They think 'cos I smile I am happy,
They don't know that I'm only a shell.
I've chosen the way that will hurt him most
So it punished me as well.

But I have this duty to others
This power which drives me on.
I find it easier to hurt you dear
Because you and I feel like one.

I think of his eyes and wonder
Just what is he thinking of me.
Does he hate me, and blame me for it
Have I made his love for me flee.

Or, has it like mine, gone much deeper.
Mine's hidden where no-one will see
If need be it's my secret for ever
'Til God takes pity on me.

Kathleen Pogson

Morning

Do I walk in your dreams as you in mine?
Never a night but smiles remembered
And words recalled are a lance to my heart.
Ah, the lie supreme! so wondrously fine -
It's you that I love and will you be mine?
And yes! I cried, because Love is blind.
But gone you were and all that's left
Is a cold clear light in an empty room,
And a heart bereft.

D Gray

In Search of Love

She wears no smile,
She tells me why:
'Joy and love
Have passed me by.
The men I know
Are full of lust
And care for only
Legs or bust.
I seek a man
Who's sweet and kind,
With love for me,
Not my behind.
Until he's found
I will not grace
With a smile,
My wondrous face.'
'Come come,' said I,
'I know you'll find
Your man who's gentle,
Sweet and kind
Now seek no more,'
Said I to she,
'That man is here.
That man is me.'

Fiona Herdman-Smith

Gold Blend

(For Collette)

How are you doing? I hope you're alright,
Now that we are passing friends,
Would you like to talk about old times,
Over coffee, in the cafe,
Just friends.

Oh, sorry, I didn't realise that you
Had someone waiting!
I smile as you walk off with him,
And feel my heart crack beneath that smile,
As I realise, I still love you.

'How am I doing?'
I still love you alright,
Even though we are passing friends.

'How am I doing?'
Would you really want to know?
Now that we are just passing friends.

My smile fades as you go out of sight,
And happy memories return, of you,
But I feel painfully empty,
As I go, for coffee, alone . . .

Michael Abbott

A Mistress

As autumn calls and summer fades
And night takes over long, warm days
I wonder how the sun will reach
That sandy, silent, lonely beach
The shadow of the single girl
- All alone, her hair flies free
I recognise her, she is me.

By day so full of life - no cares
By night alone, forgotten, empty.
Will he return, she can't be sure
Each day's a test, a trap, a lure.

To give in, care, and be held close
Or give up now and feel his ghost
Around her for her life to come
She only wants to be the one
Who fills his thoughts, his arms, his life
To be the one who is his wife.

Margaret A Casserly

The Loving

She gave you all she had -
Her tears, soft golden hair and sweet perfume -
To welcome you and bathe your weary feet.
She strengthened your faint spirit with her love.

Her love, which she had given to many men,
Was acceptable to you, and by you blessed.
You understood the longings of her heart
And sanctified her loving and her trust.

Her trust and loving, once made whole,
Became a way of life to emulate.
She followed you, and your disciples led
To live for you, accepted and beloved.

Accepted and beloved, complete I come,
To serve you truly, like the Magdalene,
All sins forgiven, purified by grace,
Needs met in full, life-love with glory crowned.

Valerie Peters

Far From Home

'You'll be going away,' said our mother one day.
For war is declared, and it's not safe to stay.
Evacuation meant nothing to me -
Except a long holiday, perhaps near the sea.
I knew nothing of heartbreak, as mum packed our bags
Barley sugar, some oranges, our names on the tags.
It just meant to me, a journey by train,
Dad saw us to the school, I guessed not his pain -
As he bade us goodbye, my brothers and I,
He had such a sad face, I did not know why.
I enjoyed the journey, laughed and talked all the way
I missed no-one then, as I recall to this day.
We arrived with our teachers, they had mentioned 'foster'
And I parted from both of my brothers near Gloucester.
I went on to Dursley to a small holding where -
My new foster parents both greeted me there.
Next day, I was homesick, I'll always remember,
I sobbed all day long, in that sunny September.
I cried for my friends, and for my small brother
I cried for my home, for my dad and my mother.
I've remembered for all of these fifty three years,
My favourite teacher could not stop my tears.
I tried to be brave, as I thought I should be,
Stayed over a year with my new family.
Dad and mum brought me home, I settled that day
And it soon seemed as though I had not been away.

M R Goddard

Portrait of a Lady

Although quite lame from early days
She'd a lover who did not falter.
The climax of her love's bright rays,
Was marriage at the altar.

With faith they started married life
Which meant quite little leisure
Her aim, to be a loving wife,
And children were her pleasure.

She gave her children, as they grew
Her love and fond attention
They gave her joy, and loved her too
The rest I need not mention.

As time went on the family grew
And soon they started working
But she was happy, for she knew
For them, there'd be no shirking.

And as she seldom could get out,
The world was brought in to her
By friends who lived just round about
By post, and those who knew her.

Then at last she illness had
Her days were nearly ended
To see her suffer, it was sad
Her fortitude was splendid.

What saintly lady could this be
No need to ask another
For let the truth come straight from me
This lady was my mother.

M Brooks

The Ending of a Marriage

Love? What caused it to bloom, to fade and then die?
Was it true? I've asked myself these questions many times.
Because you see, it happened to me.

Once I had so much, now nothing
Nothing but feelings of guilt at the hurt I've caused.
To the man I married, our families, our friends.
Regret too at never experiencing again the
Days when the children were young and our
Whole life was attuned to them.

They grew up, and the main interest we had
In common was no longer there.
Perhaps in retrospect that was when the fading began.
Now nothing, no looking forward, no planning,
To feed my creative instincts.

Just mid-air suspension, waiting for the wind
To blow me which ever way it thinks best.

But was it true? The love that bloomed?

If so, why did it fade, and then die?

Monica Helen Eveling

For you Both

Two hearts that fell in love too fast,
It wasn't destined to last,
A broken heart,
A period of time apart,
With the odd letter,
The healing got better,
I thought it was over and too late,
But then came the hand of fate,
No-one knows what the future has in store,
If in time you will love each other more,
But for now it makes me happy to see,
Your love pouring out around me.

A M Winfield

The Sands of Time

The sand is slipping out of time
Through the hour glass
Your hand is reaching out for mine
Don't let it go my lass
The life you have is all I have
To build my dreams upon
What shall I do when all is lost
And you have gone
For I am old and you are young
Don't go before your time
Reach out my love and take my hand
My life is yours - not mine

The angels came to see you
While I was fast asleep
They said you had so long to do
My love for you would keep
And when I wasn't looking
They took you far away
To somewhere far beyond - beyond
Where you will have to stay
But one day when I'm older
We'll meet again I know
We'll soar up high together
Through wind and rain and snow
When that day comes my grown up child
We'll live the life we lost
Safely in God's garden
Safely in God's love.

Gloria Rogers

A Brighter Star

If I told you of all the things I ever wrote,
The secrets of the days when we were young.
And of those nights when loving was so innocent,
Knowing that someday our star would come.

I rue the times we may have passed like strangers,
When arm in arm we could have found our way.
To promise not to lie, or ever to make you cry,
Never to see your silken hair turn grey.

As we travel along life's road,
Our hopes and dreams soar so high.
The very thought of losing you,
Can still make my heart cry.

When all the love in the world,
Cannot prevent that sigh
To be with you, to have you near,
I'll stay here 'til I die.

If you cry in the night for the love you crave,
And you think that to you life is unkind.
Through all the tears you must always be brave,
For you cannot know pain 'til your heart bleeds like mine.

So as we hold on, the stars say it's so,
That beyond the clouds your heart will be mine.
And when that day draws near, you'll know,
For a brighter star will never shine.

Terence Rainer

Black and White

I never thought
That life could be

More black and white
Than right and wrong,

Until you came along
To burn a hole in me
Which nothing else can fill;

A knot of fear,
Which is lonely everywhere
Without you,

I push you so hard,
I wonder you don't break.

Alan Dee

Nicoletta

Nicoletta, Nicoletta, dance for me, my dear.
Pirouette, pirouette, in bits of chiffon sheer.
Twirling all around me you're magic to my eyes -
Twinkling feet and arms outstretched reaching to the skies.

Your pivoting is riveting when high upon your toes,
Your tiny arms in graceful curves, Your legs in rose-pink hose.
You're like a little bird, dear - fluttering here and there,
The sunlight catching glimmers of gold-dust in your hair.

You touch your lips upon my brow when you arrive at four,
At six o'clock you blow a kiss before you reach the door.
You've come here now for five whole weeks practising each day,
You've made an old man happy - please stay, my dear, please stay.

That day you knelt beside me - I think of with delight -
I helped you with your ribbons, you said your shoe was tight -
I never touched your silky skin, you smelt of flower spray,
For fear I'd break the magic spell - you might have gone away!

Sometimes I play your music - Copellia or Swan Lake,
The shafts of light play tricks with me - I think it's you - I ache -
I wasn't really listening the day you talked of Ben,
I didn't want to hear it, I wasn't ready then.

The magic of your presence, more precious than you know,
Awoke my powers of loving - please never, never go.
Your smell of youth and freshness stays with me all my days,
So like a little butterfly when dancing in the rays.

Nicoletta, Nicoletta, must you go away?
I'll never sing another song - my heart is dull and grey.
Please shed your bits of gossamer and twine them round my head,
I never want to see again - You're leaving me, to wed!

Josie Boot

Untitled

To the movings and flutterings
deep down in my tum,
To the nearly made baby
that will make me a mum;
I love you already
my daughter, my son.

I've sat and I've knitted
sweet coats one by one,
I've schemed and I've planned -
now this part's almost done;
I love you already
my daughter, my son.

Your pram, it is ordered,
your cot soon will come;
Your daddy is waiting
for our own little one;
We love you already
our daughter, our son.

Barbara Hudson

The Day you Went Away

My life has been so empty,
Since you died in your prime,
The fact that you were so very young,
Is nothing but a crime,
But I always will remember you,
Throughout each and every day,
It seems that I am all alone,
As I travel life's weary way,
And you and I were so much alike,
It's as if we were as one,
One moment you were with me,
The next you'd suddenly gone,
And how can I not remember you,
When at each and every turn,
You move amongst the shadows,
Where the lamps of memory burn,
Sometimes I catch an echoing,
So soft that I scarcely hear,
I open a door and seem to,
Feel you instantly near,
It seems I never had the chance,
To say my last goodbye,
But I never thought we'd be parted,
I never thought you'd die,
We first met with perfect timing,
On that wonderful happy day,
But the sun stopped shining,
On the day you went away.

Mark Potter

Ben

Out of the darkness you came
Afraid of the day.
As the stars appear in the night
As they fill the sky with their light,
Out of the darkness they briefly flame
Then die far away.

Into the darkness you went
Away from the day.
As the clouds pass by in the night
So you passed at length from our sight
Into the darkness, your brief life spent
Far away, far away.

And in vain our hearts are calling
For the love that could not stay.

M Parker

Untitled

With a love so deep
I give to you
A heart so proud
to be with you
You're the best thing
that ever happened to me
My love I gave so willing and free

Keep my love, it
will serve you well
It will carry you in time ahead
through joy and happiness
Sadness and pain
and in counsel too
My love will always be there for you.

B Benedetti

Our First Grandchild

When my husband and I were told the good news,
At last it was true, grandparents to be.
Another addition to the family tree.
The baby is due in the spring they say
Plenty of time to prepare for that day.
So while we just wait for our first little treasure,
We wonder, who will it look like?
What will it be?
We're not really bothered, as long as it's bonny and healthy you see.

A few years from now,
When our grandchild has grown
We'll take trips to the seaside,
And have lots of fun,
Like rides on a donkey
And games in the sun.
Then home we must come
Grandma and grandpa,
And our little one.

The months go by quickly,
Winter to spring.
The time's getting nearer
What news will it bring.

One morning in March
The tenth to be sure.
The 'phone started ringing
About half past four.

We rushed down together,
The message had come.
Our offspring was saying.
Mum, dad, it's a son!

Joan Dewick

Dreamland

I don't believe the world is round or
The moon is made of cheese. That your wishes
Won't be granted if they don't begin with please.
That Santa lives in Greenland and rides a
Magic sleigh and leaves us what we dreamt
For when he calls on Christmas Day. I don't believe
The bogeyman will grab me in my sleep, or that fairies
Leave a golden coin for every tooth they keep. That
Witches ride on broomsticks with funny pointy hats
And turn into ghosts or ghouls or frogs or worms
Or rats. I don't believe the rainbow's end conceals
A pot of gold. That four leaf clover brings you luck or
Snowmen feel the cold. That clouds are just the
Footpath to a palace in the skies. And innocence is visible
In every child's eyes. I don't believe two lonely hearts
Should wait another day. But share a little loving if
They pass along the way. And maybe even stop to think
If they're ever feeling blue, that every star in heaven
Is someone's dream come true.

Simon Vickers